Walking with the Saints

Walking
with the
Saints

Footsteps on Ancient Paths

Cecilia Baker

Matador
9 Priory Business Park,
Wistow Road, Kibworth Beauchamp,
Leicestershire. LE8 0RX
Tel: 0116 279 2299
Email: books@troubador.co.uk
Web: www.troubador.co.uk/matador
Twitter: @matadorbooks

ISBN 978 1789013 955

British Library Cataloguing in Publication Data.
A catalogue record for this book is available from the British Library.

Printed by Printed and bound in Great Britain by 4edge Limited
Typeset in 12pt Aldine Pro by Troubador Publishing Ltd, Leicester, UK

Matador is an imprint of Troubador Publishing Ltd

Cover Image: Tana Emeny

Tom, Charles, Tana and of course Julia

Contents

Introduction

People and place. A place in Britain, say Canterbury, and a time in Canterbury, say 597 AD, and St Augustine arrives. Having reached these far-flung shores from his native Italy he walked to Canterbury.

St Cuthbert, as a young lad, had a vision that inspired him to give his life to God. He was taken in by the brothers at Melrose but ended up in Lindisfarne, thus allowing us to create a link to him by walking between the two places.

St Petroc went on pilgrimage to Rome but began his great journeys with a short walk across the Cornish countryside, to reach the coast and a ship away.

The aim of this book is to inspire people – you – to get outdoors and enjoy the countryside by walking in the saints' footsteps. My intention is, via the historical stories and vignettes that I have gathered from the lives of these people, to add another dimension to a well-known walk like St Cuthbert's Way or a barely known route such as St Richard's Way. More of us are putting on our boots and walking out; getting healthier and enjoying living longer lives. This is not a guidebook to tell you which way to go, whether to turn after the stile or take the second road on the left, etc. It tells the stories of the people in whose footsteps we follow. These are some of our most ancient routes across the countryside.

The book is a glance into the rich heritage of England via these well-documented historical figures. It aims to give people and places recognition and a story. In the early 21st century we are freer now than ever before. Our lives are longer and healthier than at any time in previous centuries. We are for the first time, perhaps ever, free to do as we please and as a society, we have the luxury of thinking about ourselves and our 'quality of life'. Walking has become one of the more popular forms of indulging that luxury. More of us are going out into the countryside and simply walking for the pleasure of it, as well as for the health benefits. Climb out of the car, bus or train. Put on comfortable shoes, take a waterproof (this is Britain after all) and start walking.

Through the detailed and intimate records we have of the last two thousand years, we know a large amount of our past. Caesar wrote extensively. Then came the Roman invasion, written about in such detail by one of the greatest historians of the age, Tacitus. He died when the occupation was still in its infancy, but the numerous letters written by his literate countrymen unknowingly continued his work. The list of historians grows long as the country grew in identity. The churchman of the 8th century, the Venerable Bede with his *Ecclesiastical History of the English People*; the *Anglo-Saxon Chronicle*, started in the 9th century and continuously added to over the centuries; Bishop Asser, also in the 9th century, who wrote as directed by King Alfred the Great; Goscelin in the 11th century; and William of Malmesbury and Geoffrey of Monmouth in the 12th. They give light to those blackened Dark Ages through the stories of the churchmen and women who appear in these pages. This book will tell a few stories of these characters and their times while walking in their footsteps, enjoying the country and getting fitter and healthier.

I was never a natural walker. It wasn't something I did for pleasure – mostly I drove cars or rode my motorbike – but eventually it became a joy. It began with a trip to Canterbury which, quite unexpectedly, started me on a journey. I am interested in far more than just walking, though. I am fascinated too by the ground under my feet. I stand sometimes, on a spot, any spot, nowhere specific, and I wonder who has stood there before. Maybe it was the site of a town. Maybe it was where a battle was fought. Perhaps a lovers' meeting place. Maybe all of the above – history is long. I write of the people who were there. We are so lucky to have so much material from our past.

So I realised very early on that I wanted three things: to feel the sun on my face, the euphoria from a good walk, and to feed my soul with the beauty of the countryside. On top of that I wanted a companion from history to tell me where I was going. In this first walk I was 'joined' by the greatest saint from Winchester, which is the starting point of the ancient Pilgrims' Way. With him I traced a little of the history of Swithun's age, as well as a few of his biographical details, and as I walked, I thought of him and his brother monks and their thoughts and pains and wishes and triumphs. In other words, I shared the road with them.

But this is really not a guidebook at all. Ordnance Survey will give you the best route you could ever need. My purpose is to share the joy of where I have been and, with the aid of my stories, to try to bring the past alive. I write to encourage you, my readers, to come out – share the sun, the rain and the great beauty of our precious isle, and feel good.

1

Walking with the Saints down the Pilgrims' Way

Hampshire, Surrey and Kent
Circa 300 to between 1536 and 154
310 kilometres
Maps: OS Explorer 32, 33, 137, 144, 145, 146, 147, 148, 149, 150, 163

Did you ever stand at the bottom of a hill and sigh? Did you think it was a bore? Just get on with it. Put one foot in front of the other, working harder – the extra effort to go uphill. And did you ever stand at the edge of a huge field and say, "What on earth am I doing here? Shouldn't I be sitting comfortably somewhere, buried deep within a book?" I did that and more. But that was before I realised just how different it could be. That was before I'd felt the immense joy, the excited anticipation, of a walk and simply loving the whole experience. The absolute freedom.

Beachy Head was a killer, a real challenge. Yes, it was a steep climb, and then there was another steep climb after that, and then another, and, good grief, don't they ever stop, these astonishing hills? They were hard work and wonderful. I loved it. The view is stunning, but for five whole miles it was just the same and after a while I stopped thinking about it. My mind was going blank – not a nice feeling. I love the walking but I realised I was missing something. I didn't understand what. It was only later that it dawned on me: I needed to know who'd been here before. I wanted to know the history of very earth I was walking over.

It was a few years ago that I found myself with time on my hands at the end of a job, and living in a city where spending money is far too easy. I needed to get out and breathe. I took the train to Canterbury. I wanted a train trip, a little sightseeing and a nice lunch, and then home again. It was one of those greyish, nondescript days, drab and chilly. By the time I reached the High Street from the train, I found it teeming with people. Mostly young students from France or Italy, but they were just so many of them. Passing through the monumental Christ Church Gate into the sacred precinct, I bought my ticket for the cathedral and wove my way through the crowds towards the entrance. Here even more were standing in groups, waiting to be told what to do. They spent their time shouting and milling around, as crowds do. I gently squirmed through them and went into the cathedral, and I was amazed how the sound from outside was suddenly muted. It wasn't quiet, but it was a hum not a shout. The huge space swallows the noise and takes it high into the vaulted ceiling towering overhead. The place is full of holy men including Canterbury's most famous, St Thomas Becket, and you can feel it somehow, immediately you walk in. Passing by the friendly volunteers, with their free handout guides and helpful suggestions, I walked into the main body of the nave and let my eyes roam about. That vaulted ceiling, so far above, seemed to reach all the way to Heaven.

Standing quite still at the back of the enormous space, I let my gaze take it all in. The whole place is worn and warm. I found myself gazing at the very ancient and beautiful 13th-century stone flooring. How amazing it felt to walk on it, and how many others have walked and knelt and prayed on this stone-and-tile floor over the centuries? The area where Thomas Becket's shrine once stood is roped off and there's nothing to see now, just the empty space. The Reformation and Dissolution by King Henry VIII in the 16th century completely destroyed all traces of his shrine, so it's been left as an empty space with a solitary burning candle. Everyone was stopping and taking photographs, and just standing, mostly in silence, looking at an empty space. *These people standing looking*, I thought, *are as much pilgrims as those from any time in the past*. Nowadays these non-religious pilgrims come not to pray, but to see. They mostly don't kiss the feet of the saints' statues, nor get down on their knees and shuffle forward in a penitential attitude to pray before the altar. They come with cameras and take pictures and wander around, but still they are there, modern-day pilgrims, and they still bring in the wealth, be it for cups of coffee and a sticky bun and perhaps a postcard, or just a souvenir of their visit. It was very restful gently wandering about in the cathedral, but my tummy rumbled and the student deluge had entered, so I exited quickly.

I wandered the High Street in search of a nice place for lunch without too many people; that failed. But in my wanderings I came across the Pilgrims' Hospital, officially called the Hospital of St Thomas the Martyr of Eastbridge. Ignoring my hunger pangs I ducked in; it was a low entrance. The place was deathly quiet. Utterly empty except for the man on the door, who asked me for £2 to help with the upkeep of the place. It was a tiny and cool underground room, almost a crypt. It embraced me. It reached within me. I walked around in the profound silence, letting that feeling sink in, and felt slightly irked when a couple came in to look too. They didn't even talk – they just looked – but I wanted to be there alone. I left.

However, it was too early to go home after my lunch and I was soon walking again. I saw a sign pointing southward out of the city. It was pointing out the path of the North Downs Way, and also a section of the unknown (to me), ancient Via Francigena, the French Route. I loved the sign. A small figure, somewhat hunched, with a little kerchief bag slung on a pole over his shoulder and a walking stick, heading towards a blue shape with yellow stars which, I guessed, meant the Continent. How romantic, and how ancient, and how exciting.

Without much of a thought, I began to follow the signs and came across a wonderful, tiny, ancient church on the route called St Martin's; somewhere, I guessed, where the pilgrims would come and pray for safe deliverance for their journey to Dover and beyond. It was easy to follow the route and soon I was out of the town and passed a neatly harvested field and a stretch of woodland, and before long I reached a tiny hamlet with another church. Another prayer stop for the pilgrims, perhaps, and somewhere to light a candle this time? I walked down small lanes to out-of-the-way places, through the pretty Kent countryside, listening to the birds singing and enjoying being in the fresh air. Soon I had walked a few miles and it was getting quite late in the day, and eventually, when I spotted a train station, I went home. I had, quite simply, loved walking there very much, and I knew I had to go back.

I was intrigued by that figure, with his swag bag and walking staff, of this Via Francigena. The first mention of an actual pilgrim route was in documents found amongst the papers of an early Archbishop of Canterbury, Sigeric the Serious. Why he is called Serious we don't know, but it could be simply a derivation from his name from the Latin. He was on his way to Rome in 990 to collect his pallium (the sign of office, a stole) from the pope. Having made his way there, he stayed an extraordinarily short time (some say three days), then headed back and made a note of his route and where he stayed. He crossed France, Switzerland and Italy, just under two thousand kilometres all told. I wonder if he walked or just rode his donkey all the way?

The route, or routes, as there was never one single road like the M1, was already well trodden from the earliest of times, by traders and travellers as well as by pilgrims. It was more heavily used after about 1000 when Europe quietened down from the constant tribal wars. Then pilgrimages became very fashionable. The paramount destination for a pilgrim was, of course, Jerusalem. One route there, and perhaps the safest, was overland via Rome and then a ship to the Holy Land from the heel of Italy. It was also quite feasible to sail all the way, picking up a ship anywhere along the Mediterranean coast. However, most everywhere was crawling with pirates and, when the winds were in the wrong direction, it would have been jolly hard. The long land route through the Balkans and then Turkey and south was very perilous, until King Stephen of Hungary's father converted to Christianity in 985, which then allowed Stephen to Christianise the kingdom in 1038. Long before that in 636, Christian Jerusalem had fallen to Islam and hence was dangerous to travel there at all. So as an alternative pilgrims travelled to Rome - to the mother church and the tombs of the ever-popular saints Peter and Paul.

The first pilgrimage route was referred to as Iter Francorum in the *Itinerarium Sancti Willibaldi* of 725, the itinerary of Willibald, the Bishop of Eichstätt in Bavaria. The first mention of the actual term 'Via Francigena' was in 876 in a parchment, the *Actum Clusio*, found in an Italian abbey. However, it is only because of Sigeric and his retinue's diligence that we know anything about it today. His diary manuscript was found in the British Library by a researcher in the 1980s. Sigeric and his party, though, were just the ones who wrote it all down. We can only guess how long people had been walking along those paths – maybe for countless millennia.

The big thing about walking is the freedom in one's mind. It ranges over every subject without really dwelling at length on anything. I find myself constantly being brought back to the now, to check on my path, to brush the cobwebs off my face, or simply on hearing a bird calling nearby, or a rustle in the bushes. But then I'd be thinking about the feet that had trodden this way before me. I had gone back to my road out of Canterbury and had reached the coast at Dover down the Via Francigena, but now what? I wanted more – I wanted the 'spirit' of the walk to carry on, but I didn't know why. Just walking for the sake of walking suddenly seemed pointless.

I walked the South Downs Way along from Eastbourne. It was wonderful to walk over the beautiful chalk downs of the Seven Sisters. But something was missing. I simply wasn't called back to that route, but I was to the rest of the Via Francigena over on the Continent. However, I feared the enormity of that walk; walking all the way to Rome. It would be expensive, it would take a lot of time, my feet hurt etc., etc. It was such a colossal enterprise and I was very unprepared. *Not yet*, I thought; *one day, but not yet*. So I looked elsewhere, closer to home, and found the Pilgrims' Way. This, I realised, would work. It is well documented. It is easy to do in short stages and it has such a lot of history. However, to bring that history to life I needed a companion.

I found my companion with St Swithun. He is the obscure and relatively unknown 9th-century Archbishop of Winchester. He was chaplain to King Ecgberht of Wessex (802–839), and also the tutor to his son Æthelwulf. When Æthelwulf became king in turn, he kept Swithun as his archbishop. Swithun was well known for his church-building and for his charity, and after his death his relics became a magnet to the sick for their healing powers. His only documented miracle while still alive is peculiarly mundane. It seems some rough workmen smashed an old woman's eggs for the sheer fun of it just as Swithun was walking nearby. He picked up the eggs and, lo and behold, they were all intact and not broken at all!

The only reason we know of him, unlike many of our early saints, is the weather. According to an old nursery rhyme if it rains on the 15th

July, Swithun's feast day, then it'll carry on raining for the following forty days, and if not then there will be drought, also for forty days. There is a legend wherein his intercession was successfully invoked. Queen Emma, mother of King Edward the Confessor, called on Swithun in her hour of need. She was in bad grace with the king, who claimed she preferred the children of her second marriage to him, as well as giving him insufficient support when he became king. He took all her possessions and accused her of being too friendly with the Bishop of Winchester. As punishment for her 'crimes' she was ordered to undergo an Ordeal. But when she walked over the red-hot ploughshares, she cried out to St Swithun and all was fine – no burns, no pain, nothing. Following his death in 862 Swithun's head was detached from his body and sent to Canterbury Cathedral. Very medieval. It has been assumed that he went on pilgrimage to Canterbury, according to the custom of the time, but it is also believed that he accompanied King Alfred the Great on his first pilgrimage to Rome, when Alfred was still a very small child. The path between Swithun's see in Winchester and the great cathedral at Canterbury is called St Swithun's Way until Farnham in Surrey, where it becomes the North Downs Way. It follows the ancient route through Surrey and into Kent. This, I felt, was a good walk.

I had an afternoon stroll with my sister on the Itchen Way into Winchester up from Southampton. What a wonderful stretch of meandering, gentle river – narrow, shallow and very inviting. There were willow trees overhanging the banks and I spotted a kingfisher dashing through the branches. Dogs were jumping in and chasing stones on the riverbed. Children were squealing and splashing around, jumping into the deeper pools. It was sun-dappled and lovely. I was sold.

But before I could simply stride off into the distance, I wanted to know more about Swithun. I visited his church, the cathedral at Winchester, which is breathtakingly magnificent. Again, those tiles – so beautiful – and again, I was hit with the profound consciousness of those people with greater faith than mine, who worshipped here begging for help, or thanking with grateful praise for some fulfilled prayer. Swithun's tomb is new. He was buried originally in the old Saxon church, but some hundred years later his remains were removed from his tomb and his relics displayed within the church. When the Norman cathedral was built in the 10th century, the relics were rehoused in a magnificent shrine and became a great draw for pilgrims. Following the Dissolution his relics were lost, but now there is a new shrine to their eponymous archbishop. The Winchester Cathedral website tells the story of how the nursery rhyme regarding Swithun came about. When he was dying he asked to be buried where he could be stepped on by the faithful as they entered the cathedral. When he was moved into a gold and bejewelled reliquary a mere hundred years later, it is said he was angry and caused a terrible storm that raged for forty days.

It was early in the morning – quite chilly for late summer, but I knew it would warm up. I stood at the front of the cathedral and looked for a sign indicating the Way of St Swithun. Not a sign from God, but simply a sign with the direction to walk. Nothing. Surely, I thought, there would be something for Swithun's Way here? So I looked around with greater zeal, but still there was nothing to show me the route out of town. I popped into the still-empty cathedral, and the kind woman organising herself for the start of the tourist day didn't know either. Oh. I stood for a while and considered. I sort of guessed the general direction and walked north-east, and promptly lost myself in the smaller roads away from the centre – roads made higgledy-piggledy with new housing estates and a leisure centre. I asked a girl walking her dog if she knew of the route to the next village on the Way; she didn't. When I explained I was walking St Swithun's Way, she knew immediately.

The route was very overgrown, and I did wonder if it was right after all. Obviously not many people walk this way any more. I found the river, the one I had enjoyed so much south of the city. Here it was all bog and boardwalk and I meandered through endless fields, some with cows and some without. All the time I could still hear the rush of the motorway. The road is undoubtedly the more original way, but St Swithun's Way parallels it faithfully if noisily. The Pilgrims' Way is, however, a fake. It's a modern route based on ancient paths. The truth is that it is the creation of an enthusiastic Victorian surveyor, who wrote a pamphlet called *The Pilgrims' Way in West Surrey* in 1871. He marked it on an Ordnance Survey map, and so here it is. Before that the paths would have been walked for time immemorial. As Hilaire Belloc and others have pointed out, the topography of the route from the Channel to the important pre-Christian religious sites in the Stonehenge area is one long chalk ridge.

I may have been walking with the companionship of Swithun, but I was completely alone. I saw no one, walking or otherwise, until I came to St Swithun's Church in the small village of Martyr Worthy a few miles out of Winchester. It was standing neat and square in a small well looked-after graveyard, raised high on an embankment of some kind. As it came into view I had to look up at it, as though on my knees in worship. I went in, delighted that the door was open, and there was a stained-glass window of the saint himself. Outside again, I greeted the woman – at last, a person – who was rebuilding the drystone wall surrounding the graveyard. She didn't seem inclined to chat and after a gentle hello, she slowly picked up a stone and studied it from all angles, before selecting another to place very carefully and exactly. Wonderful to watch, and so peaceful too. But I didn't hang about as I was rather keen to get on. I had many miles to go and was still quite uncertain of my way.

Every now and again I would see a sign fixed to a tree or a gatepost, pointing me onwards. Sometimes it was not for St Swithun's Way but for the Itchen Way, but since they were one and the same for most of the route, I was content with that. The route was caught between the road and the river, so it was only a matter of not walking into someone's house or finding a brick wall in the way. I did walk around a huge field twice before I fought my way out of it, only to fall onto the road, which was ghastly, so I forced my way through a few hedges to escape the mad rushing of vehicles. They seemed like aliens mindlessly rushing by. The fearsome noise, after the quiet of the woods and the riverbank, was intense. Eventually I reached my destination for the day, my first day on the Pilgrims' Way, and with aching feet I went home.

My immediate goal was Farnham, the end of St Swithun's Way. I spent three days walking through sometimes boggy ground, fields and woods through some of the prettiest parts of Surrey. I tried to keep Swithun and his fellow pilgrims in my mind. What would they have been thinking about as they walked, I wondered? Robbers? Food? Sore feet? Prayer? When I told my friends about my walk, many asked if I wasn't scared. They said they'd be frightened to walk alone. I thought about it as I walked, but thankfully our world is safer than in years gone by. As for food, the bushes were full of berries and I had to control myself to avoid stopping and feasting on every ripened bush. Sore feet? My sympathy was with those pilgrims, although they spent much more of their lives walking than we do. Prayer? What is prayer after all? I thought about the path under my feet. I thought about the next gate to open, the next turning to take, about the blue sky and calling birds and the buzzard circling. I thought about everything and nothing. One day as I was thinking (and not thinking) and walking, I was suddenly aware of my father walking next to me. I was talking to him and listening to his reply, although I could hear nothing. It was extraordinary. My father died a few years ago. I felt he was with me, and it made me feel good.

The last few miles to Farnham were marvellous. The fields of barley had been harvested and I could make out the tread of other walkers across the large, open fields. The sun was shining and the skies were criss-crossed with contrails, making lovely patterns in the sky. I walked for a while with the only other walkers I had come across so far on my journey – Debbie and Geoff. How many miles did they have under their feet? This was a gentle day out for them, with Debbie getting used to two new knees. She was sanguine about them. She had played squash furiously and had been obsessive about her aerobics and was paying the price for it now. I admired her spirit. I wondered if I would rather have sat in a squashy armchair and read a riveting book instead of walking. As I walked the last stretch into town (alone now since Debbie and Geoff had gone for the bus), through a wheat field ripened and ready for harvesting, I met a girl out walking her dog. She walked with me for a while and asked about my journey, and said she knew nothing of the Way. She seemed keen to try it herself. It lightened my spirit to chat to someone so enthusiastic.

In the 1960s two men, Alan Blatchford and Chris Steer, met up and walked together, and in the course of their walks they dreamt up a plan for a walking club with routes all over the country. They created the Long Distance Walkers Association with Alan's wife Barbara in 1972. By 1978 they had completed the trail and launched the North Downs Way. Perhaps it should have been called the North Hills Way, as 'downs' is the Old English word 'dun', meaning hill. Anyway, it follows more or less the same direction and path as that the pilgrims of yesteryear would have followed. However, since this is easy walking ground and the most direct east-to-west route it makes sense that through these valleys and along these ridges was the equivalent of a modern major highway; perhaps a route that our Neolithic ancestors trod. This was my route too; I was walking in the footsteps of those ancestors.

Farnham is a thriving market town with a maze of old streets, many of which have been turned into pretty pedestrian areas filled with cafés and shops, and it has a good railway link. It was mentioned as being quite wealthy in the Domesday Book of 1086, and in the Middle Ages it had a rich wool market. Its greatest period in history, though, was the English Civil War, when it played host to both the king and Oliver Cromwell. The day was overcast but warm as I climbed out of the train onto the platform at Farnham Station. I found my first waymarker as I headed away from the station. It was so well marked. Clear, obvious signs; I barely needed my guidebook's instructions. The book did tell me of the local flora and fauna, though, which was great. Such a huge change from the beginning of St Swithun's Way, where I was fumbling about for the trail. Here it was blazoned. It was good too to be able to think of other things rather than wonder if I was totally off course. (I have since found a very good guide to St Swithun's Way, published by the local county council. I had failed to go into the tourist information office in Winchester. My loss.)

The route took me through many stretches of woods of beech and oak, ash and hornbeam. The ground was littered with beechnuts amongst other things, crunching under my feet. The beechnuts were very useful on the muddy parts of the track. I saw huge horse chestnut trees towering majestically above the beech, and I picked up lots of conkers – throwing one away when I saw another, more gorgeous. The beech woods were very beautiful with the sunshine dappling through the branches and onto the carpet of fallen leaves – the overcast day had turned into a gorgeously sunny one. As I walked alone I could hear only the distant hum of the road; a noise that never disappeared but sometimes grew stronger and sometimes faded. Suddenly I heard a great rustling from the undergrowth not far from me, but I couldn't see anything in the tangle. I wondered what could make so much noise. Then I remembered that wild boar had been accidentally reintroduced into the woods of southern England, and on top of that I was pretty certain one of their favourite foraging snacks was exactly what I was walking on – beechnuts! I was excited and just a little nervous to come face-to-face with a wild boar. Sadly, though, it turned out to be a fat pigeon trying to get itself loose from some sort of entanglement in alarm at my approach. How disappointing... but I think I'll get a whistle, just in case, to scare anything away in the future. Not long after this I came across three men felling trees in the wood, so the chances of boar in the vicinity would be non-existent. Oh well.

So I walked through nature reserves and small villages, on towards Guildford and its important river crossing. I was walking parallel to the Hog's Back that carries the major traffic, but I didn't go into the town. I assume pilgrims would have stopped for the night, or for a meal or to buy provisions. But maybe not, if the town wasn't sympathetic to them. Now the route stays further south, going through the suburbs and then back into yet more woods. The track had changed from the sandstone I had been walking on, to the chalk of the North Downs. I liked the sandstone when it was hard and compacted, but for the last couple of miles before Guildford it had been a bit like walking on a beach. I had just passed by the Watts Gallery and up a bridleway that was just a very narrow, sunken lane, when I got such a scare. Being that this was such soft sand I didn't hear a huge four-wheel drive approach until it revved right behind me. A trifle mean, I thought as I scrambled up the steep edge, but I smiled broadly and waved; not such a good idea as it turned out as I slipped and nearly ended up under its back wheels!

Anyway, the soft sand was slowly giving way to hard chalk. Past Guildford, I walked up into more trees in Chantry Wood. The woods were more open and the paths more defined. It wasn't until I came out of the woods, at the top by a church, that I realised people still come for the church and for the truly awesome view. The church, which was locked up tight, was called St Martha's, as was the hill. I did read in the guidebook that some Christian martyrs had been killed here, so its original name was more probably Martyr's Hill not Martha's Hill. The sky was beginning to darken nastily, but the view was incredible to gaze out over southward.

For some time I met no one as I continued on into the woods again, until I came across, quite fortuitously when I needed a second opinion, a professional dog walker parking up to exercise a gorgeously shiny black Labrador. I had finally come out of the woods to find several paths in front of me. I hadn't realised that I had been walking on a sort of parallel path to the Way, but I had in front of me two directional signs, which were a puzzle. I asked the dog walker, who hadn't a clue, but she did point out the general direction of the next village that I had on my map, and that was enough.

The path turned northwards along a road, then plunged back into the woods, to go on climbing up onto a higher ridge leading up to the top of the North Downs. Now the sandstone was completely gone, and the chalk was hard beneath my feet. I was walking on a broad track. The path became more distinct the further along it I went. I came across a large, round concrete water tank. I wondered who had built it. I reckoned not farmers, as animals wouldn't be able reach in to drink. They would have fallen in and drowned. Apparently this 'road', I found out eventually from an information board, was where the Canadian Army had been based as they trained for the D-Day landings. The water tanks were theirs.

By now the weather was not cheerful at all. Initially it was only a light drizzle, but soon I could smell the rich wetness of the earth and hear the patter of falling rain on the leaves high above me. I was footsore and getting a bit cold, so as I passed West Hanger and on to Hackhurst Downs I decided it was time to go home. Eventually I found a small byway called Beggars Lane to take me off the route. It was so steep I had to use my walking stick to stop myself sliding downhill. It was practically sheer. And it didn't stop. On and on it went down. I hadn't realised just how high I had been up on the scarp of the downs. Then it got yet colder and darker, and the rain started. The lightning flashed and the thunder roared. It rained, hard and straight down. I cowered under my umbrella beneath a tree. The whole sky was black – it looked as though it was staying forever. *Oh, well. I'll dry eventually*, I thought, so I tramped on – literally as my soggy boots made a sort of squelching noise as I made my way to the closest railway station. As I approached it, though, the rain suddenly stopped and the sun sprung out, and it was all quite wonderful as I climbed onto the train, delighted with my walk and being able to dry out and get warm again on the homeward-speeding train.

I rejoined my route at Box Hill and Westhumble. I was the only person getting off the almost empty train. Gosh, it was a lonely place. There was no one there at all. No station attendant. It was a dark day again, and cold as I walked down the road and under the rushing motorway to reach the start of the next stretch. This time, though, I was slightly better prepared: I'd brought my pink poncho, so I was all covered up and it was nicely warm. The route began with some stepping stones over the River Mole. I heard the river before I saw it – also rushing like the motorway. It was very full, and I could only just see the stones under the water. Luckily in 1992 the Friends of the North Downs Way had put up a footbridge so I managed to get across and stay dry.

The next challenge was Box Hill. Apparently there are 267 steps to the top. So much nicer than scrambling up the steep and slippery hill. For all that it was very much worth the climb to reach the top. Standing next to the trig point was glorious. The sun had come out and mist hung in the valleys in amongst the treetops. It was fresh and clean and green and beautiful. A man ran by; the thinnest man I'd ever seen. He was in running kit and covered in mud. We called a greeting and I warned him how slippery the track was, and he thanked me and agreed. I thought no more of him as I walked along eastwards, through yet more gorgeous woods. I followed the signs, although here there are so many public footpaths it sometimes got confusing. There were far more people within earshot at this popular spot.

Soon I lost the sounds of other people and some miles passed under my feet, wet and muddy now, until the path levelled out and here I came to the real, naked chalk of the North Downs, bared by the feet of thousands of walkers. *Good*, I thought, *no sticky mud*, so I strode on and promptly slipped over. It was as slippery as ice. It was ghastly. I stopped in a very narrow part to ponder if I could step on something not so lethal when suddenly, and right in my ear behind me, a voice said, "Hello." I nearly died – I certainly leapt out of my skin. It was the runner. He had run around Box Hill, he said when I asked him, and added that he was on his way back home, which was my destination of the day – and it wasn't even midday yet! The shame of my day's slow walk to his half-day's fast run! I let him pass and watched as he gingerly trod on the chalk before finding a better footing further on, and then he was gone. Phew. What hard work for him. Not so much for me, though. I much preferred to gaze at the scenery and smell the roses, so to speak, on the track. I was in no hurry. I was loving where I was (apart from the chalk) and what I was doing.

I was in a dream from then on, as I got into broad woodlands – sometimes oak, mostly lime with a wide and easy path – and I was thinking of the changing seasons and the darkening sky. I forgot to worry about the route as the signs pointing out the North Downs Way were pretty numerous, and anyway, so many feet had passed this way I could simply follow the most prominent path – or so I thought. Somewhere in the woods it occurred to me I hadn't seen any of those signs for a long while. I realised I had done it again. On such a well-marked trail I had yet again seemed to have missed it. I wasn't lost as such, but I wasn't on the right track. I checked my map and saw I was paralleling it again. The real Way had taken a sharp uphill track to reach the ridge, while I had gaily walked straight on and was skirting the bottom of the down. Darn it – I hated the idea of retracing my steps, so I decided to walk on. Surely the paths would meet eventually.

The rain, by this time, was again more serious. It was so dark that I wondered if the day had slipped by and it was actually getting towards evening. My watch, when I looked at it, said it was only 12.15. Serious weather. I had just spotted a track up the hill when the rain came down. It was incredibly heavy, beating down with such ferocity that the water was bouncing back up to my knees. Again I found a large tree to cower under, hoping it would pass soon. It didn't, and I was very impatient to get back on my track so, with pink poncho this time as well as my umbrella, which is purple, I started upwards. But oh no – the path was all chalk. For about four hundred yards I crawled up the chalk in the pouring rain, brambles tearing at my poncho and forcing me to close my umbrella. It was all very inelegant, if colourful, but I was sure there was no one to see me as I puffed and panted my way up.

I was incredibly pleased to reach the top. Out of the brambles I came and onto grass – so easy to walk up now. There at the very top, on the ridge, was a man standing with his bicycle in the torrential rain, wet and muddy but completely unconcerned about it, staring at me as I appeared out of the bushes. He commented on how steep that hill is and how impressed he was that I'd even attempted it – that made me feel all warm inside. We stood for a while, still in the rain, and discussed the weather in a most English way and enjoyed the clearing view stunningly laid out before us. The dark clouds above were just breaking away to the south and a much brighter sky was following them, but I just loved the way the rain meant nothing by now. Some things were greater than the discomfort of being wet, like that view and a friendly chat with a muddy cyclist. I said goodbye to my wet cyclist friend as he pedalled off in the opposite direction and I slogged on. A little further on in a car park by Gatton Park I came across, to my great pleasure, a kiosk selling hot drinks and it had a bit of a roof with a seat, so I had the best cup of tea ever and only the second sit-down of the day, in the dry, and I was happy.

There are lots of lovely little villages dotted around the countryside, and one of them is Merstham. It's very pretty and old. One dated building told me it was built in 1796. I set off through the village in the early-morning sunshine. It was cool and the mist hung around the tops of the downs above the village, caught in amongst the treetops. The trees were just beginning to change to their autumnal colours – all very soft and gentle. I had to walk through a narrow passageway to cross over the main road – I dislike walking through these narrow tracks so early in the morning as they are always full of night-time cobwebs which stick to your face, and I'm left wondering where the spider has got to – in my hair? However, they're not tarantulas, nor funnel-web spiders. I dare say the spider minds more than I do. It's sticky and yucky, though.

Crossing the noisy and busy road again (I was beginning to hate this road – all roads, really), I came across the 13th-century church dedicated to St Katherine of Alexandria, who was a 4th-century martyr. Parts of this church are Saxon. I believe a lot of these old places of worship are built on powerful ley lines that cross all over the countryside. People have been drawn to these specific spots for centuries, and I think there has to be a strong reason for that. So, with a little prayer I strode on into the still and increasingly humid morning.

Along this stretch I came across a ruined tower, a folly. It was the Whitehill Tower, according to my book, which was built by a grieving father for his son lost at sea in 1862 – very sad. Even sadder, though, was a photograph pinned to a nearby tree showing a small white Chihuahua. He was lost, and his owner was offering a whopping £1,000 reward. That is some well-loved dog. Written on the poster was the plea *Help us look for our precious boy*. I saw dozens of these posters for miles around. I just hope they found him.

Sometimes the woods opened up and I saw marvellous vistas away off to the south and, nearly always below me, the Pilgrims' Way. Mostly it has become the monstrous motorway which growls and roars away below the ridge, constantly reminding me of how much I'd have liked to hear the birds sing and wind rustling the leaves – sounds simply drowned by our everyday lives. This part of the Downs has been quarried extensively and I had to detour around a large disused quarry, which brought me within touching distance of the racing cars before I could cross over and walk away south, to reach Oxted. It sounded a pretty wealthy sort of place in the Domesday Book of 1086, and even now as a commuter town for London. It is full of million-pound homes tucked away behind high walls and manicured gardens.

So on I walked into Kent, which turned out to be just like Surrey. I was walking along paths crossing farmers' fields. Mostly they were bare of crop, or just the tailings from the harvest. But they were so wet that walking along the paths meant either sliding through grey clay mud, or deep puddles. Many feet had tried to walk along the edges of the paths and had widened them to their furthest reaches. Usually they were bordered by brambles or deep ruts filled with water. I wished I'd brought my wellies at times, and all thoughts were concentrated on staying upright. I thought neither of the pilgrims, nor of the birds, nor anything else. No point in hanging about, though, so I ploughed on only to find my way barred. Not only were there signs telling me that the way ahead was not a public footpath, but there was absolutely no right of access and I must keep out and was on CCTV. I was surprised until I looked at my map. I found I was standing at the back of the Foreign Secretary's official country residence of Chevening. I took the hint and walked on through yet more fields and cowpats. These fields did at least have some cows, actually young bulls. I'm always wary of boisterous young bulls, but these were far more interested in eating as much as they could to take any notice of me. I was pleased to veer away from the high ridge soon after Chevening and came down a fantastically steep field, which allowed me a glimpse of the house itself in amongst the trees.

Nearby lies the very important Church of St Botolph. St Botolph was a Saxon abbot in 7th-century East Anglia. The town of Boston in Lincolnshire (and subsequently Boston in Massachusetts) was originally called Botolph's Town, as it is believed that he was granted land there to found his monastery. He is the patron saint of wayfarers and travellers and his church, sited right on the Pilgrims' Way at this point, was a very important stop. I'm sure that St Swithun himself would have been more than welcome here. According to my book the church has eight bells, two of which were cast in 1715, which is quite impressive. Pity I didn't get to hear them. Maybe I wouldn't have been able to anyway, as yet again I was down walking next to the motorway before being able to cross it and walk into the little town of Otford.

The name itself is a shortening of Otterford or Offa's Ford. King Offa, of the great Offa's Dyke between Wales and England, was the King of Mercia who fought a battle around here in 776. Now it's a charming village around a pond swimming with ducks, and has lots of little cafés and ancient-looking pubs. It even boasts a Roman ruin to show off its age, which would have already been just rubble by the Middle Ages.

As I waited at Otford Station for my train away from the route for a night's rest, I wondered what other pilgrims thought about as they walked, and why they walked too. Pilgrims journeyed for an awful lot of reasons, many of them nothing to do with religious fervour. Chaucer's *Canterbury Tales* is a brilliant window into the lives of medieval people. As a poet he no doubt exaggerated the characters, but for the most part it's thought he was describing real people. The Wife of Bath with her early brusque feminism, the miller, the cuckolded husband, and the cook whose story was so offensive he was cut off in midstream – none of these seem to burn with the religious fervour that we nowadays associate with pilgrimages. They were travelling in Chaucer's time in the 14th century when there was a huge surge in pilgrimages. By then the undertaking had changed into something quite different to the early pilgrims' journeys. Life in the Middle Ages could be described as hard and brutal, and often rather short even if one made it past babyhood. Maybe pilgrimage could offer a ray of hope and inspiration, adventure and reward to their otherwise dark lives.

Long before the Middle Ages, as far back as the 3rd century, the *Itinerarium Burdigalense*, the Bordeaux Itinerary, recorded the journey of an early pilgrim from Bordeaux who crossed Italy to Constantinople, Turkey and Syria on his way to Jerusalem, and then returned via Macedonia, Otranto and Milan. Then the focus was on pilgrims wanting to walk in the footsteps of Jesus himself, so all the routes led ultimately to the Holy Land.

The first really important pilgrim (both historically and contemporaneously) was the mother of Constantine, the Emperor of Rome. The Edict of Milan in 313 made Christianity legal throughout the empire, which, to a large extent at the time, was the world. Before the edict Christians had been persecuted and killed, but Constantine promoted religious tolerance for all. His mother, the Empress Helena, travelled to Jerusalem in 326 where, amazingly, she found the True Cross of Jesus, the cross that was used to crucify the Son of God (or so she was told and believed). She also persuaded her son to build the Church of the Holy Sepulchre, which is still a magnet for pilgrims from all over the world. Others, following her example of bringing home holy tokens, claimed to have found parts of the saints, for example the thumb of St John the Baptist. Queen Matilda of England owned the hand of St James of Santiago, although she herself didn't travel to the Holy Land. This encouraged others to seek out relics of the saints, but those that couldn't or wouldn't undertake such a long and dangerous journey still wanted to see them. This inspired shrines all over medieval Europe, and they quickly became very popular. In this nasty, brutish world, before the science of nature was understood, medieval people were incredibly superstitious. They thought that anything that went wrong in their lives was down to the wrath of God. If the harvest failed, it meant God was angry. If the cow didn't give milk, it meant that God was angry, and worst of all, if anyone fell ill it meant that that person needed to plead with God for forgiveness for whatever misdemeanour had made him (or her) so angry. Some form of penance, therefore, was needed. One form was, of course, paying a sum of money to the Church. Another was going on pilgrimage to a shrine to beg for forgiveness of a particular saint – or rather, I suppose, to ask that saint to intervene on their behalf with God. As to the choice of which shrine to go to, there is no record of one saint at being better at, say, curing leprosy or a broken heart than any other.

It appears that the choice was down to the fashion of the day, who was in vogue at that moment, and some saints were more enduring than others. It looks as though Swithun was one of the more enduring ones, like St Thomas of Canterbury. Strangely enough, though, there are records of the sick often apparently getting better when they reached the shrine, and hence they were said to have been 'miraculously' cured. It is possible that this could have been down to a change of diet. Areas around the shrines, the towns and the countryside, were usually wealthier because of the money brought by other pilgrims. Hence the food may well have been of better quality, so it could have been that something as simple as moving to another area was beneficial. Sometimes it wasn't only the quality of the food, but also crop diseases. Ergotism was a huge issue throughout the northern swathes of England and the Continent. We understand it now, but they didn't have the slightest idea of its existence in the past. Ergotism is the poisonous effect that comes from eating rye infected by the ergot fungus. This fungus forms on grasses, and especially rye, after wet summers. In the Middle Ages, when many summers were very wet and the sickness was rife, the 'infliction' was called St Anthony's Fire or Holy Fire. The symptoms are either convulsions or gangrene, both of which are fairly horrendous. Medieval people would have had absolutely no way of understanding the correlation between the bad summer weather and the disease. All they knew was that when they visited shrines, especially those closer to the Mediterranean and its drier climate, they would get better. So when large quantities of people got sick in an area, a town or a village, it led to mass pilgrimage to shrines, often those of the Blessed Virgin Mary. This was the case in England and northern France, as was witnessed by one Hughes Farsit in 1128. By moving to land where there was no ergotism, the pilgrims were all cured by the miraculous intervention of the Blessed Virgin Mary.

But pilgrimages were also undertaken for reasons other than asking for God's help or forgiveness. Some simply wanted to get away for a bit; have a break from their normal humdrum lives and get a bit of excitement, or get away from a difficult spouse or overlord. Or maybe they just wanted to go on holiday. Life must have been pretty dull in the enclosed societies of small villages where most people were born, lived and died and never ventured further than the next village. Travelling to faraway places for a long period of time would have been very enticing to some; early adventure tourism.

Another reason for going was imposed by the authorities, usually a bishop or a prior, as punishment. Penitential pilgrimages were established as early as the 5th or early 6th centuries when members of the clergy committed some heinous crime like murder, incest or bestiality. The Church demanded what was in effect a period of banishment. To travel without comfort or ease, or even in chains and barefoot, usually at colossal personal expense, to a shrine that was perhaps hundreds of miles away, would be dangerous and difficult, but it was a suitable punishment to atone. Some pilgrims had to 'wear' the weapon they used to commit the crime – e.g. their sword strapped to their bodies. For some more minor crimes a fine would be sufficient, but if the crime were too great, say for murdering a bishop (which appears to have been quite popular), then not only would a fine be demanded but the murderer would be banished as well. To add to the banishment, the severity of the crime was taken into consideration when it came to deciding which shrine the pilgrim needed to go to. If the crime wasn't really bad, then a local shrine would suffice as punishment. However, if it was really appalling then the pilgrim would have to go all the way to the farthest shrine possible, and sometimes to all the major sites of Europe – Canterbury, Santiago, Cologne and Rome – which could take several years.

The pilgrim's passport also evolved as a result of this. It was one thing to be ordered to go off on pilgrimage, but there was no means of checking to see if that pilgrimage was carried out. There is a record of a murderer who was ordered to Santiago but left Paris, travelled about twenty miles down the road, then turned back and went home. So, to ensure good conduct and that the punishment would be fulfilled, the Church authorities demanded evidence of the journey as well as the arrival. Hence the pilgrim's passport was created. It had to be stamped at official stages along the route, and a testimonial had to be issued by the local authorities of the shrine at the final destination. Only when these documents were produced back home was the punishment deemed to be completed. Modern pilgrims also have passports and are usually proud to have their passports covered in stamps from everywhere – shops and cafés as well as cathedrals – and the testimonial on arrival. Unlike today, however, in the Middle Ages a pilgrim would have had to seek permission to leave their home to go on pilgrimage and in 1388 King Richard II actually made it illegal to go abroad without a passport. On the plus side, though, the passport would usually accord the bearer an easier passage and cheaper food and lodging, as today's pilgrims also enjoy, especially on the Camino-to-Santiago route.

I arrived back in Otford fairly early one morning, when everything was still very sleepy. A few commuters were about, and in the car park I saw a group of walkers gearing up for a day's walk – perhaps they were going my way? They were very busy amongst themselves and still had a lot to do, so I didn't go over and chat. Instead I forged on straight up the hill, back up to the top of the ridge to Otford Mount. I wound my way through woods with their thick underlay of fallen leaves, across a few narrow lanes with their speeding cars, and skirted several soggy fields. At one stage I came out of the woods to admire the magnificent view south, and in front of me was a very large cross. I was by Oak Hall, which had originally been Otford Manor, built for the sugar magnate Sir Oliver Lyle in the 1930s, but now a centre for Bible studies. It is in a lovely part of the world.

The path wound on through more fields and more woods paralleling the Pilgrims' Way, below which at this stage was a narrow, pavement-less lane. I stopped for breakfast in the cool morning air on a huge felled tree trunk by a narrow, sunken lane. Overhead, I heard parakeets squabbling. They are noisy and aggressive and, as much as I do like them, I'm sorry that the native birds get chased away by them. Still, I wasn't expecting them here. Soon after I heard more usual sounds – the raucous call of the crow and the chatter of magpies – but still no smaller birds. Horses are very popular here – most large farms I came to had one or two in an adjoining field. As I walked on, I crossed a number of fields with their occupants grazing quietly away, sometimes raising their heads to see who I was. I was enjoying the fields and the silent companionship of the horses; no walkers even here. Suddenly the path turned down the scarp again to rejoin the Pilgrims' Way. The road had become a bridleway. Lovely shaded walking, but soon my peace and quiet were shattered by two men on trail bikes who literally flew over the brow of the small hill in front of me. I shrank into the hedge to let them pass, and I did get a thank-you. Soon after that I heard a noise behind me and glanced back to see two runners – I stood aside for them too.

On I walked, enjoying the sunshine and the steady rhythm of my steps. Eventually, of course, the path turned another sharp corner and climbed steadily up, back to the highest ridgeway, up and up sometimes so steeply the path turned into steps. I was in Hognore Wood, where my guidebook warned me to watch out for cyclists who favour these steep downhills. I saw no one until a fellow walker came towards me down the path. He was dressed in green plus fours; polished, well-worn boots, muddied but still polished; and carrying a hardy, proper backpack. I was ridiculously pleased, when we stopped to chat, to realise he had his sweater on inside out, as I was feeling so very badly dressed compared to him. He mentioned he'd walked the North Downs Way several times, usually with four friends, one of whom was eighty-four, but he was beginning to slow down. He himself admitted to being in his late seventies. I'm sorry we weren't going the same way, as it would have been lovely to chat more. If we had met fifteen minutes later on my walk, and earlier in his, we could have had a cup of tea together. The North Downs Way took me through the Trosley Country Park, right past to their teahouse. I had to stop. It's an impressive teahouse. It boasts all sorts of green credentials. It has award-winning toilets, a water-recycling system, natural ventilation and a living green roof, which I admit I didn't see, but I'm sure is lovely. The path through the park was actually on the route, so it made for a 'stroll through the woods' that was most agreeable.

I was now in perhaps the least populated part of the walk, despite being in one of the most populated parts of the UK. I started walking up a forest track with lots of felled timber lying about, and dead machinery too. Another trail bike came down the track towards me. The rider had to stop to open a gate, and he sweetly apologised for the noise he was making. I heard him almost constantly as he enjoyed the forest paths all around me. I walked on a few more miles before entering thick, ancient woods. Known as the Rochester Woods, they're extensive and quite claustrophobic. I loved it when the sun was shining, but not so much when it didn't. Then it felt quite foreboding as well as claustrophobic. At one point the sun disappeared and I came across a huge, black-barked tree. It was very spooky. It was an enormous oak tree and its branches seemed to angle up in a most peculiar way. But the thing that really struck me was its blackness, its truly black bark. I had instantly the strongest thought – *It was here that they used to hang witches!* Oh, fanciful thoughts. I laughed at myself, slightly nervously, and walked on with perhaps a greater turn of speed. Therefore, when two cyclists sped up from behind me, I wasn't in the least unhappy to see them. Silly.

Still slightly spooked but endeavouring to shake it off, I was glad to come out of the woods into a lovely sunny field. At the end of it I found a signpost and realised I was well over halfway to my destination: 114 kilometres already walked and sixty-nine to go. Swithun would probably have been very pleased to know his journey was nearing the end. This small village I had come to near the waymarker was called Cuxton, after a Saxon man called Cucula. He had a stone named after him, and the name seems to have stuck throughout the ages from Cucola's Stone, to Cuclestone, to Cookstone and now Cuxton. The villagers have placed a large stone by the scout hall to commemorate Cucula. Archaeological materials, mostly hand axes, found hereabouts suggest that humans have lived in the area for around 200,000 years. That's a good long time. These hand axes are now on display in the British Museum, such is their importance. Nowadays it's a regular small village with a Co-op store and a school and lots of houses bunched around the village hall. It sits just off the main road to Rochester, on the banks of the River Medway.

From here it's a short walk into Rochester. This was the biggest place I had come to after Guildford, and it dominates the countryside. I walked back up from the village to the ridge through thin woods and onto open farmland before coming back down to the railway cutting, and the 'funnel' into town over the river. Rochester was also a place of pilgrimage, not only to rest before going on to Canterbury, but also as a shrine in its own right. After 1201 it became quite big. In that year a pilgrim called William of Perth was on pilgrimage to Canterbury. He had with him a foundling boy, whom he had found on his doorstep as a baby and raised as his own. As they were leaving Rochester after a few days' rest, this orphan foundling took William on what he claimed was a short cut to Canterbury. There he hit William over the head, stole all his money and took off. William's body was found by a madwoman who, the story goes, made a garland of flowers. This she placed on the corpse's head and then on her own. Miraculously, she was cured of her madness. Such a marvellous miracle was worth promoting. William is now called St William of Rochester and is the patron saint of adopted children, which seems slightly perverse considering his end. His shrine was second only to St Thomas Becket's for a long while. It is still possible to buy medals and pendants with an image of him. Medieval pilgrims would have been able to buy exactly the same sort of thing.

I found the cathedral at the far end of the high street, just across the road from the rather formidable castle, standing on a rise overlooking the river. A cathedral has stood here since 604 according to the cathedral's history. The 7th-century English monk and historian the Venerable Bede mentions Rochester in his *Historia Ecclesiastica Gentis Anglorum* (*Ecclesiastical History of the English People*), which he completed in 731, one year before his death. He wrote that Justus was consecrated as Bishop of Rochester by Saint Augustine himself, who was the first missionary to bring Christianity to the Saxon world from Rome. A monastery was founded here in 1082 and was in existence until the Dissolution. Usual story. Now it's a soaring part-Norman, part-Gothic, very light place of worship, and a stopping-off place for tourists. It has a really beautiful organ placed right in the heart of the church between the congregation and the choir It was the light that was so special. With the huge windows – now plain glass but they would have been stained glass originally – it lets in so much daylight. I wandered around with a few other sightseers with their cameras and, to my delight, found myself walking down the Pilgrims' Steps. They are now covered with wood to preserve the ancient stone treads, which have been worn away by literally thousands of feet coming to pray.

William's canonisation to sainthood, I'm afraid, strikes me as a bit of cashing in on the pilgrim cash cow by the medieval church. There were rather too many saints who suddenly had shrines dedicated to them, who would cure the ills of pilgrims. Every shrine needed pulling power and, unlike St William and his local miracle, it was usually a relic of one sort or another. Over the centuries there were so many pieces of the True Cross produced that it must have been truly gigantic, not to mention the phials of breast milk from the Blessed Virgin Mary. Records show that there were lots of clergy and laymen who were sceptical of many of these miracles, but the enormous wealth brought by the pilgrims was very tempting. St Thomas at Canterbury was one of the greatest saints, and his shrine drew literally thousands if not millions. As a result, Rochester would have been quite eclipsed due to being so close. So much the better, then, if they had a saint of their own, so the pilgrim could drop in for a few days and perhaps buy a trinket or two before going on – just, I suppose, as I had done. I had a cup of tea rather than a trinket, but nonetheless I brought in some wealth.

Putting my scepticism to one side, I said a prayer and lit a candle in William's chapel before moving on. Getting back to the North Downs Way proved interesting. I took a bus to what I thought would be a convenient point to connect back with the trail since the route doesn't go into Rochester town itself. When I was dropped, though – in the middle of nowhere, but in between a busy A-road and the motorway – I was utterly disoriented and walked about in circles until I actually stopped a car to find out where I was! To my embarrassment, the trail was right next to me. So, thanking my saviour, I trudged on to face the motorway. This was such a cacophony, and it didn't lessen for many miles. It isn't just a motorway and a busy A-road, but also a couple of train lines, one of which was the high-speed track down to the coast. I had to cross the Medway on the same bridge as all of these, and it was just so loud. I quickened my step and was practically running to get to the other end. As usual, the Way has formed the base of modern routes, so the most traditional trodden path (or bridge) is now under the rails and roads. Eventually I was taken high onto the Wealden Ridge overlooking the noisy bridge and the river, with some lovely views into the mistiness of the lower ground. Now I was truly in the heart of Kent and its tiny villages.

I passed through the village of Detling that has been subsumed to a large extent by Maidstone, making it more or less a suburb. The wood now was an open pine one and the ground was soft to walk on, with a deep layer of soft needles. Bliss. It was incredibly steep and as I gingerly made my way down, watching my steps with great care rather than rushing headlong, I missed the sign again and, though I should have stayed on the high ground, found myself at the bottom of the scarp once more. I had landed myself on the Pilgrims' Way and not the North Downs Way. As I negotiated my way out of the bramble field I'd found myself in, I began to wonder if I was actually meant to walk on the Pilgrims' Way instead. I kept finding myself on it without meaning to – was I drawn to walk it? Well, no point in fighting the inevitable. One advantage of several was the view. While high on the ridges I had been mostly in woods. They are very pleasant, but one rarely gets a glimpse of the sky. The occasional panoramas were a treat, but I love big open sky and walking on the Pilgrims' Way, I could see much more of it. I found myself on a very narrow and quiet road, mostly left in peace but for a few men dressed in tight Lycra whizzing past on expensive bikes – all very serious and businesslike. I met one walker with a backpack who told me at length of the delights of the pub in the next village. I think he'd spent quite a bit of time in there. When I reached the village of Thurnham, I found the pub without difficulty as it was smack on the road, the wonderful-looking 18th-century Black Horse Inn. I'm sure it was a welcome break for footsore and weary pilgrims.

The route went on straight ahead for a few more miles. I was still walking on tarmac, and I realised it was a mixed blessing. It was nice not to have a kilo or so of mud attached to one's boots, but the hardness of the metalled road was not kind to the feet. I did enjoy the open skies. At one point I paused to watch a bird, perhaps a skylark, mobbing a much larger kestrel. They wheeled about the sky in a sort of ballet, the small bird shrieking all the while and the kestrel very calmly turning another slow circle just out of reach of the panicked bird. The Way stretched on for a few more miles and eventually I came to the village of Hollingbourne, and another pub – The Dirty Habit; referring to their clothes, of course. Its website says that monks used to brew ale here in the 11th century and *gave rest to weary pilgrims*. King James II is said to have stayed here on his way to France, too. The village is again a tiny remnant of what it must once have been. Near the pub is a large manor house, now separated into flats, and an old church full of illustrious dead. That's about it – oh, and a train station as this is again a commuter town for the London magnet, where I took myself away for the night.

Rejoining the path the next morning, I again passed The Dirty Habit and was cheered on by local people enjoying the cool, sunny morning. The Pilgrims' Way continues through open fields until it joins a bridleway enclosed by a mixture of hedgerow bushes, which eventually turn into an avenue of trees. The path continues along the edges of several fields as it winds east through the countryside. The fields were all bare as I passed, waiting for the next harvest. The early morning had brought on the first frost, but it soon burnt away. I walked past the small village of Harrietsham and found myself coming up to the gate of Summoner's Farm. The thought had occurred to me a few times, as I came across all these houses called Pilgrim's Rest or Pilgrim's Whatever, that it's a pity they don't offer hot tea on a cold day, or even fresh water. It wouldn't have to be elaborate – perhaps a thermos on a small table, similar to those where people sell their extra vegetables or eggs by the roadside. Perhaps there are simply too many walkers? Maybe, although as usual I was alone.

Soon, however, I came across *Percival*. He isn't a person, but he looks like one. *Percival* is a wooden sculpture of a pilgrim monk taking a well-earned rest; in fact he seems to be sleeping. I sat down next to him on his bench and sympathised with him that someone had appeared to have stolen his nose! *Percival* looked quite resigned to his loss. We sat together for a short time, in harmony with the pilgrimage as well as the sunshine. Eventually, I felt *Percival*'s progress to Canterbury was rather slow, so I wished him a good pilgrimage and said goodbye. As his plaque read, *Pilgrim bound with staff and faith – rest thy bones*. I had rested and now, with my walking stick – *my staff of faith to walk upon* – I moved on.

I tramped on, passing the village of Lenham. I would have missed it entirely if I hadn't come across a vast white cross, carved into a sloping hill as I walked through an enclosed nature reserve. It was the Lenham Memorial Cross, created in the 1920s for those killed in the First World War. During the Second World War it had been covered so it didn't become a beacon for enemy bombers. In front of it they had put up a bench, which for some bizarre reason they had fenced in. Why? A mystery. The village of Charing, soon after Lenham, is where many pilgrims stopped before making the final push on to the shrine at Canterbury, now only a few miles away. Charing is very pretty, and old too; it is recorded that there was a market here in the 13th century and a fair in the 16th. I'm certain that St Swithun would have come here. Again, records show that land in Charing was given to the Christchurch Priory in Canterbury in the 8th century, and by the time of an Archbishop Peckham in the 13th century, there was an important Archbishop's Palace right next to the church within the village. It was one of several that had been constructed specifically for pilgrim archbishops during medieval times. Apparently King Henry VII stayed here, as did his son Henry VIII when on his way to meet the King of France at what came to be known as the Field of the Cloth of Gold. After the Dissolution, the Crown leased the land out for farming and the palace itself became simply a manor house. Now it is partly a ruin, covered in very attractive ivy, but many of the original buildings still stand including the charming palace cottages, tucked into what I had assumed was the ruined wall but I now think was the original gatehouse to the whole complex.

I walked on into the church and stopped as I opened the door. Someone was playing the organ. I closed the big, heavy door as quietly as I could. I couldn't see anyone playing, and I wondered if it was a recording. As I moved towards the altar I spotted a woman sitting behind a small organ off to the right. She had a mirror angled to see the vicar for her cues during a service, so she knew I was there. Her playing was really lovely, and I enjoyed it very much as I knelt to pray. It added to the atmosphere of the old, cold building. As I left she started playing *It's a Long Way to Tipperary* for Remembrance Day. I hummed the tune for the rest of the day! Outside, I found two people planting small crosses in the ground next to a wooden crucifix for the Remembrance Day parade. As I walked away from the church and down to the village for a cup of tea, it occurred to me that I had completely forgotten to look for the stone, somewhere within the church, which is supposed to be the stone that John the Baptist was beheaded on, donated by a returning Crusader. Gruesome.

I really liked Charing, despite the stone. I stopped off at the only tea room I came across and popped my head in before going in, to ask permission with my dirty boots. The landlady said she didn't mind a bit. It was a cosy little front room in a Tudor-looking house with low ceilings and a fireplace big enough to crawl into, full of chintzy tablecloths and home-made cakes. The tea as always was yummy, and I had a really nice chat with the only other people enjoying a cup. I had followed them, at a distance, for the last half-mile of the route into Charing. We talked of our walks and I was quite jealous that he was a botanist, so could spot all the flowers etc. that I knew I simply missed completely. So, despite being only a short distance from Canterbury, I took the train away for the night before the last stretch.

Onwards from Charing for the push towards the end, I walked on over much of the same ground, over the Westwell Downs and Eastwell Park, in the fading light of what were by now much shorter days. I stopped at the extraordinary ruin of St Mary's Church in Eastwell, right next to the entrance to Eastwell Manor, now a hotel. The bright winter's light was shining on the large lake right next to the church, giving the place an almost surreal presence. It is rumoured to be haunted by the spirit of a long-dead monk.

As interesting as it is, it doesn't compare to the tomb of Richard Plantagenet. Francis Peck, in a two-volume book called *Desiderata Curiosa*, which was published in the 1730s, described him as Richard the Master Builder or Richard of Eastwell. He was supposedly an orphan and handed to a Latin schoolmaster who brought him up. When he was a teenager he was commanded to go to the field of Bosworth on the eve of the great battle, where he was taken before the king. The king, Richard III, told him he was his bastard son. Young Richard was told that if his father won the field, he would acknowledge the boy as his own. However, King Richard lost, and the young lad fled back to Kent and lived a secluded life. He only told his story as an old man when he was questioned by a new lord of Eastwell Manor. He was buried in the church, where his memorial still remains. It has also been suggested that maybe Richard was one of the Princes in the Tower, the young Duke of York, who obviously decided that being a master builder was preferable to being a prince or indeed king. It was truly one of the most evocative places on the whole journey.

So now I was on the final stretch, and this is where the Pilgrims' Way and the North Downs Way part company. Back in Boughton Lees village at the start of the day, I got off the bus and looked around for the path. Just then a man walked by with a terrier that decided to make friends with me, so I asked (the man, not the dog) if he knew the route. Not only did he know, but he gave me great directions uphill and round bends and warned me where the worst mud would be. He mentioned too to watch out for the split in the two paths. A few hundred metres out of the village is where the paths finally diverge. He said to be aware as the divide is simply a gap in the hedge. No fanfare, no trumpeting, just the gap.

Well, it wasn't quite that bad. I found the gap, and it did have signs. So, waving a mental goodbye to the North Downs Way, I strode off east. I walked down a well-used track and, crossing a field, came to the older branch of the village, called Boughton Aluph, with its 13th-century church, All Saints. Wanting to see if it was open, I walked all around the church and found three small doors, but no main door. How odd. Surely I must have missed it, so I walked around again. All the doors were tiny and locked. The most interesting thing about the church, besides the lack of a main door, was the buttress propping up one corner. It was obviously shifting and had been for several centuries. Away I walked, shaking my head at its oddity, to King's Wood a bit beyond Boughton Aluph. I had read that the pilgrims had gathered in Charing to wait for *a goodly number* before facing the King's Wood, where the danger was too great for lonely travellers. I've read since of another wood that I have walked through that had a similar reputation for robbers: the Alice Holt Forest near Winchester. Here, during the famous St Giles Fairs in Winchester, guards were sent to patrol the woods and protect travellers. Apparently in 1282, King Edward I ordered that roads should be cleared up to two hundred feet on either side to stop dastardly people from leaping out from behind a bush.

The King's Wood in front of me was a huge, dense wood that pilgrims had no option but to pass through. But, of course, it was a haven for robbers. This was the most dangerous part of the whole pilgrimage. I was alone, but I think the risk of robbers now is fairly slim. Also, I had read that over a thousand wild boar live in the wood. Aha – another chance of a boar sighting! Now I had my whistle I was on the lookout for one. So up I climbed into the wood, a steep, winding path through a farmer's field. As predicted by my friend in Boughton Lees, it was incredibly muddy. Because of the trees it had no chance to dry out, and I had to literally pull out my boots from the mire with every footfall, making sucking noises as I did so. I made slow progress. I was concentrating on my feet so much that if a boar had happened to come by I would have missed it anyway. As I walked through the wood, with trees and bushes butting right up to the narrow path and not two hundred feet away, I did look back a few times just to make sure that there were no robbers, nor boar, tailing me, but thankfully for the former and sadly for the latter, there was nothing. I was, as always, quite alone. About the only wildlife I ever see on my walks are grey squirrels darting out of the way.

The wood went on forever, until eventually the path petered out and became more solid. I heard barking. An eager spaniel galloped around a bend towards me in greeting, followed by a female voice calling out that he wasn't dangerous. A spaniel, dangerous?! Delightful. She had more dogs in her pack: a couple of Labradors, a poodle I think, a rough-haired dachshund and several others of indeterminate heritage. She had in total about eight dogs, all boisterous and fun. I was wearing my pink poncho now as the rain had outgrown the fine drizzle of the early morning and become a downpour. The dogs were most excited by the flapping of the poncho.

The rain became even more torrential as I climbed the short, steep hill up School Road into the main square of Chilham village. What a really beautiful place. If it hadn't been raining it would have been even better, but I didn't stop to stare for long – I spotted a statue of wet, huddled pilgrims so, after a swift photo, I bolted into the church for a brief respite from the elements. It's a shame, though, as the square is bordered by Chilham Castle on one side and the most charming historic inns and shops all around. It's worth a longer look. Another time.

I didn't want to linger at this stage and I walked on through the graveyard, and up again to the truly extensive apple-growing regions of Kent. The orchards went on for miles. Not only was I walking next to them, but also through them for ages, and on one farm I walked past the mobile huts for the migrant workers who flock in every picking season to shift this mighty amount of fruit. The season was well over now and the huts empty, but many of the trees still had fruit on them, and I wondered if they'd mind if I picked some. If I had been hungry perhaps I may have done, but I wasn't, so I didn't. On and on they went, and I walked in sunshine and showers through them, getting closer and closer to my goal. As the day wore on the rain clouds moved away and the sky cleared, allowing the sun to shine on me. Finally I could take off my flapping pink poncho and enjoy striding quietly through the countryside. I walked through the curiously named No Man's Orchard Nature Reserve, which I assumed meant apples for everyone, and entered the ancient Blean Wood and came across an Iron Age hill fort called Bigbury. The trees here have been felled and it's given archaeologists the chance to really explore the whole area.

This last stretch proved very hilly and my legs were tired with the constant uphills in slippery mud – two steps up and one slip down. I was getting closer and closer. The roar of the big A-road, which fed into Canterbury, grew alarmingly loud and eventually I had to cross over it. One more steep downhill and across a small stream, then a steep uphill and there – I was on a driveway which fed, via a couple of small lanes, to a roundabout and the London-to-Canterbury road. So busy. *Whoa, people, calm down.* People walking towards me no longer caught my eye and smiled and wished me good morning. I was back in town. *Look down, don't catch anyone's eye.* A bit sad. I crossed the great divide of the busy roundabout and walked down the street to St Dunstan's Church. Now I was in the true town. The road is bordered by offices and lots of B&Bs, for the thousands of people who come to Canterbury to study or visit. I've no idea how many take the time to visit the ancient church dedicated to St Dunstan, but if they don't they miss something special. St Dunstan was a 10th-century Archbishop of Canterbury and his church was the first shrine that pilgrims visited on arrival, so naturally I had to stop too for a prayer and a look-see. St Dunstan was canonised in 1003, very soon after his death in about 988. He was England's favourite saint, and his the most visited shrine until Thomas Becket's. He was born very near to Glastonbury, the son of a nobleman. He was well educated and in time went to court to join his uncle, who was then Archbishop of Canterbury. Dunstan eventually took holy orders and moved back to Glastonbury, but remained influential with royal matters. He was involved with organising the coronation for King Edgar, and in actually designing the coronation crown too. The foundation for modern-day royal coronations still incorporates the spirit of his plan. A second famous saint is attached to the church too – the head of St Thomas More is in the Roper Crypt, safely laid in his son-in-law's family vault by his beloved daughter Margaret.

One much-publicised miracle was attributed to St Dunstan after a visit to his shrine. After Becket's murder and canonisation, King Henry II came down to Canterbury on a sacred pilgrimage in penitence for the murder. It is said he wasn't keen to, but things were going rather badly for him on many fronts. His various wars with both the Scots and the French were going badly and, worst of all, he was very unpopular with his people for what he had done to their archbishop. So he rode down to Canterbury and stopped at St Dunstan's Church, as he was obliged to do by ancient custom. He took off his fine clothing and donned a sackcloth-and-ashes shift, and removed his fine shoes too. Barefoot, he then progressed through the streets to the cathedral before prostrating himself before Becket's tomb and praying all night. That very night the tide turned for him in both the wars and his people's favour. St Dunstan's reputation was firmly established.

I kept my clothes and especially my shoes on and walked down Watling Street, one of the extraordinarily straight roads created by the Romans for their marching soldiers, and entered Canterbury by walking past the West Gate. Almost there. I wound my way down the main street. It wasn't as crowded as when I had been before at the very beginning of this adventure, and I walked by the inspirational Pilgrims' Hospital. I thought for a nanosecond about going in but I was so keen to reach the cathedral I didn't want to waste a second, so I carried on until I reached the tiny lane leading to it. As I came around the corner the sight of the great Christ Church Gate and the cathedral behind was bathed in sunlight. Magnificent. The students were not so numerous here today, and it was easy to get to the ticket booth. A young man leant out and I told him I had come for a blessing. He pointed out the Welcome Centre where I needed to ask, and when I came to pay he waved me through.

The Welcome Centre was almost empty except for one woman and her son. I waited until they had finished talking, whereupon the centre woman turned to me and asked, "Are you a pilgrim?"

I stopped for a moment to think and hesitantly said, "Yes." At that, the woman and her son suddenly whipped around and also asked if I was really a pilgrim. "Well, yes. I suppose I am," I said. The son, who was looking highly embarrassed and obviously wished to be miles away, was doing a school project on pilgrims and they had been hanging around most of the day hoping a pilgrim would turn up! And here I was!

The mother fired her questions at me in quick succession and I was rather startled by it all. I'm afraid my answers to the questions were not good. I think I may have added far too many miles to the total when she asked, and I was a bit hesitant when she asked me why I had done it all. I needed to sit down and ponder that, but I gave her answers for her dying-with-embarrassment son who was lurking behind a pillar. Eventually she finished her rapid-fire questions, asked my name and shook my hand and congratulated me. *Phew, that was intense. But what a welcome.* Suddenly I felt proud and pleased. I hadn't expected anything and here I was being greeted as a celebrity – well, not really that, but it was nice anyway. Now I could think about the blessing. The Welcome Centre woman was sweet too, and also shook my hand in congratulation, and gave me a small certificate with the date to commemorate my arrival. Unbeknownst to me, Canterbury Cathedral does now issue pilgrim passports, but since I didn't have one this was as much as I could get. I wasn't complaining at all – I was really pleased.

I entered the cathedral slowly. As I crossed the porch it had suddenly hit me that I was about to rush in, so I slowed my pace and walked in deliberately. A dean was standing just inside the door to greet visitors, so I asked her if she could bless me. She could, and she was delighted. Her name was Rosemary and I was the first pilgrim she'd been asked to bless, and she was quite excited by it. She gave me the option of being blessed wherever I wanted in the cathedral.

"Oh, golly. Um, it's a big place – what do you think?"

"Well, maybe by the new stained-glass window, or on the worn Pilgrim Steps, or in a private chapel or the crypt?"

The crypt seemed a quiet place, and away from the sightseers as I didn't really want to be a spectacle, so we made our way to the tiny, empty Chapel of the Holy Innocents in the crypt. There Rosemary asked me if I would like to pray for anyone or anything especially, besides my pilgrimage. I mentioned my nephews and nieces, and she gave me my formal blessing and left me alone with my thoughts.

So, it's done. Canterbury is the end of the Pilgrims' Way. I have walked all the way from Winchester and I am pleased with my achievement. I never doubted I would, but I'm a bit surprised I have.

I wandered about the cathedral for a while and got one of the helpers to take a photo of me in the nave as proof – all filthy and dishevelled – and I bought a hat with *Canterbury Cathedral* written on the brow. A cup of tea in the cathedral teashop and a scone in celebration, and then home via the train full of well-dressed and clean commuters on their way home.

2

Saints in an Early Age

Cornwall
5th century
Fifty kilometres
Maps: OS Explorer 106, 107, 109

The Middle Ages may have been the apex of the fashion for going off on pilgrimage, but the paths to holy places by holy men and women were well trodden centuries before. In fact, the period between 450 and 600 has become known as the Age of the Saints.

The first of several Roman invasions of the British Isles was led by Julius Caesar in 55 BC and then continued more enduringly in 43 AD, under Emperor Claudius. Rome was always keen to expand her empire and Britain was reputed to be a rich land in both tin and silver, as well as good soil for growing food. The local Britons, however, put up a stiff fight, invariably calling on their gods to help them in their defence.

The Romans believed that by destroying the Druid priests and 'conquering' the local gods their conquest of Britain could be realised.

They saw Wales as the key, and fought hard, bloody battles to wipe out the Druids who would give their blessings to the many rebellions against Roman rule. So, in 60 or 61 the Roman commander Gaius Suetonius Paulinus attacked the island of Mona, now called Anglesey. This had long been regarded as the spiritual home of the Druids. It was a total massacre, basically destroying the whole Druidic caste. The Romans didn't really care how many gods the locals worshipped so long as they included the Roman gods too.

The worship of one Christian God probably seeped into the British Isles with the traders and merchants from the Continent. Then when the Emperor Constantine announced the Edict of Milan in 313, Christianity became widespread. Early records show Christians here before 313 too, when Christianity was regarded as just one of the many cults that proliferated throughout the Roman Empire. At the Council of Arles in 314, three bishops from Britain are known to have attended, including Restitutus, the Bishop of London. One of the earliest Christian martyrs in Britain was the former Roman soldier St Alban who, according to the Venerable Bede in his *Ecclesiastical History*, was executed in 302. By the middle of the 4th century, Christian places of worship were to be found throughout the country.

Later, when the pagan Anglo-Saxons invaded Britain following Rome's departure, Wales and Ireland and the far south west of England, what is now Cornwall and Devon, became strongholds for the religion. In those areas, largely cut off from the rest of the country, it developed into a more home-grown Christianity, a Celtic Christianity. (Although it must be remembered that there was no organisation of the Church in Britain; the term is used purely to describe a difference between this Christianity and Rome's.) This Celtic Christianity evolved over time, developing certain rituals that differed from Rome: the fixing of the date of the Easter celebration being one example, and the monks' tonsure for another. Celtic Christianity grew rapidly and was obviously successful as the Venerable Bede writes of a monastery in Wales, at Bangor, that was so large it had been divided into seven with at least three hundred monks in each part. Eventually in the 6th century Pope Gregory I in Rome sent a mission to convert the Anglo-Saxon Britons under the leadership of Augustine. This changed the face of Christianity in Britain. But the worship of the one Christian God was well established and had been for several centuries, and one holy man who helped its development, or at least influenced it, was St Petroc, patron saint (or one of them) of Cornwall.

He was such a well-known saint that there have been many books written about the holy life of St Petroc, or Petrock, or Pedrog, or today he might be called Patrick. However, it is just possible that the stories of at least two people called Petroc have been conflated into one person. What is recorded is that he was abbot of Lanwethinoc and his dates are c. 468–564, and that he is regarded as the most famous saint of Cornwall, although there is quite a line-up of Cornish saints. Petroc was reputed to be the son of a Welsh King, named in the 12th-century *Life* (known as the *Gotha Life*) as King Glywys of Glywysing, and to have had twenty-four brothers. When the king died, the people of Glywysing wanted Petroc to take his father's place. However, he preferred the monastic life and travelled with several others to Ireland to study theology in the famous colleges there.

Eventually, after some years away, they returned to Britain and came ashore at Hayle, in the mouth of the River Camel in Cornwall. ('Hayle' in ancient Cornish simply meant 'mouth of a river' or 'estuary'.) One source (c. 1366) quotes John of Tynemouth saying that, as Petroc and his followers arrived and disembarked from their primitive craft, they saw some locals working the fields. St Petroc asked them politely what religion they were, and they replied rather rudely, and said they were thirsty and that he, as a holy man, should provide a drink for them. He struck the ground with his staff and a spring of fresh water gushed out. They were astonished, and told him to seek out St Samson of Dol, already a famous holy man in Cornwall and, like Petroc, the son of a Welsh nobleman.

St Samson sent him off to the hermit St Wethnoc. St Wethnoc was another holy man living in a cell nearby. Wethnoc greeted Petroc and, after spending just one night in Wethnoc's cell, Petroc decided it was the perfect place for him to stay. Wethnoc realised how holy Petroc was, and that his arrival was fulfilling an ancient prophecy of a very holy man of great sanctity, who would come from Ireland to magnify the name of the Lord. Anyway, Wethnoc gave up his cell to Petroc. In return, he asked a favour: he wanted the area around his cell to bear his name. Petroc was glad to grant this and named it Llanwethinoc. Unfortunately for Wethnoc, its name is now Padstow, derived from Petroc's Town.

So Petroc lived in this cell for thirty years until one day he and his followers decided to go on pilgrimage to Rome. Not much has been recorded of his first visit. On his return, though, the weather, as soon as they arrived back in Cornwall, was terrible. Petroc rashly said that the following day would be fine. Unfortunately, it rained for the next three days. Petroc was appalled that he had been presumptuous enough to assume he knew God's plan, so disgusted with himself that he decided to turn right around, there and then, and go straight back to Rome.

He didn't stop there, though. After a time he travelled on to Jerusalem, to walk in the footsteps of the Lord, and then further on than that, too. He must have enjoyed the life of a pilgrim, as it is recorded that he turned east after reaching Jerusalem. On he walked and, facing many perils, he arrived at last on the shores of the Eastern Ocean, where he promptly fell asleep. One story has him waking to see a tiny vessel drifting towards him, just big enough for one person. He climbed in, and without any means of propulsion but the waves, fetched up on *a certain island* where he spent seven years fed by a single fish, given to him at intervals, by the Lord. It is recorded, less curiously, that he spent seven years in India, and eventually returned to Cornwall with a wolf he had befriended there. The tame wolf must have made quite an impression on the Cornish folk when he got home.

The train moved slowly to settle next to the small platform, with its dilapidated bridge, incumbent café and small ticket office, at Bodmin Parkway before coming to a jarring halt. It stopped only briefly to allow a small handful of people to climb off, and then it slowly, very slowly pulled away, sighing slightly in the cool afternoon air. I sat in the café and had a cup of tea, waiting for my walking companion, my sister, to join me, and for the next bus to Padstow. I got chatting to the rather bored lady behind the counter who told me that the 14.30 bus that I was hoping to catch was cancelled and so the wait would be rather longer. My sister duly arrived on time and as I was telling her the news a bus came in, so we dashed for it. It was going only a small part of the way, but it was better than waiting at the station, so we climbed aboard.

It did go only a short way – just one stop. Here we waited patiently, with me wondering if we could go and explore around the town. As we were discussing it that supposedly cancelled 14.30 bus hove into view. Fantastic, but it was not all smooth sailing then. I realised after about an hour or so that we must have reached Padstow, and I expected a bus stop, but the next thing I knew, we seemed to be heading away. I leapt to my feet, raced to the driver and, yes, that had been Padstow! We grabbed our packs and climbed off and started walking – slightly sooner than anticipated!

Petroc is not to be confused with St Patrick, who drove out all the snakes from Ireland, although Petroc was friends with St Samson who is credited with ridding Cornwall of its last serpent dragon (see story later). Thomas Fuller, churchman and historian, did describe Petroc as the *captain of Cornish saints* in his work *The Church-History of Britain*, written in 1655.

St Petroc's bones are no longer in Padstow where they were originally buried, following his death in 564. Here, he founded a monastery, which survived and thrived for centuries. It was only in 981, when the Vikings attacked Padstow and destroyed the original monastery, that the monks moved further inland to Bodmin, taking the bones of Petroc with them. The name 'Bodmin' means 'sanctuary of the monks'. There they founded a priory.

Petroc's bones have moved about quite a bit since then. In 1178 a 'disgruntled' priest of the priory called Martin stole them and took them off to Brittany, to the Abbey of Saint-Méen near Rennes. Naturally the prior, Roger, asked for them back, and when the Bishop of Exeter and King Henry II intervened as well, they were returned but minus a rib, which was left in France. The king gifted a rich reliquary for the relics, which were venerated in Bodmin Church until the Dissolution. Luckily, before the reliquary could be destroyed or taken off to Henry VIII's coffers, it was hidden, walled up in the porch. It was only found again in the 19th century, and was then put on display in St Petroc's Church in Bodmin. But it was still not safe, as quite recently in 1994, thieves stole the reliquary and caused a terrible uproar. Prayers were said for its return and even Queen Elizabeth II made an appeal to the robbers on its behalf. Thankfully, they were found in a field in Yorkshire and duly returned to Bodmin, but no doubt security is somewhat tighter than before.

Padstow is a delightful town, nestled in an elbow in the estuary of the Camel River, away from the direct winds and waves of the open sea. The tide was out and the beauty of the great stretches of sand was outstanding. A gloomy and cold wind chilled me to the bone as we walked along the headland before fish and chips in the local pub and settling into our cosy B&B. It didn't take long to sort our kit before a good night's rest in readiness for our walk along the pilgrim route of the Saints' Way.

The Way follows in the footsteps of St Petroc from here on the north coast of Cornwall down to the southern port of Fowey, to where he probably took ship to go on his way to distant Rome and Jerusalem. Early the next morning, as soon as St Petroc's Parish Church threw open its doors, we went in to look around this 15th-century version of the earlier church. Petroc is shown in the stained-glass window, with a deer standing next to him. He is credited with converting King Constantine of Dumnonia, the all-powerful monarch who, while out hunting one day, chased down a deer that took refuge in Petroc's cell. Petroc refused to allow the king to kill the deer, and even managed to convert the king to Christianity there and then.

The Saints' Way starts at the door of the church, and going down the path, we went through the lychgate. A lychgate is the covered porch on entering the graveyard surrounding the church. They were used for the dead before burial. Bodies were kept here on a cart or bier, usually wrapped in a shroud and attended by bodyguards to stop it being stolen, until the burial ceremony, which often started from the lychgate before going into the church. Here we found a map of the route and the first of the clear waymarkers going south.

What a wonderful morning to walk. It was cool but not cold, with a very slight breeze but no sun. The sky was heavy with cloud, casting a murkiness on the view. The route climbs immediately from the lychgate up to Dennis Hill, which is a high promontory overlooking the mouth of the River Camel, and the site of an ancient Iron Age fort. A good lookout for those raiding Vikings, too, we thought. Dennis Hill and the obelisk that now stands here, put up to celebrate Queen Victoria's jubilee in 1887, leads up and over the hill to Little Petherick Creek, and what a lovely view greeted us here, with the creek and the route ahead of us.

Nowadays this is open farmland and is partly covered by gorse, but in those far-off days of the saints, it would have been practically all wooded. Down by the side of the water, walking next to the creek, it was likely very marshy and wet. Now there are boardwalks and good paths and, besides the odd fallen waymarker post, including one that had been well chewed by a bored horse, the going was easy and swift. Nearby were silver, lead, and copper mines that together employed as many as forty men in their heyday. The mines were abandoned in 1872 because competition from foreign mines made it uneconomical to carry on here.

In a very short time the tiny settlement of Little Petherick appeared, with a few houses and a bridge and, of course, a church. This is the second church dedicated to St Petroc and is referred to as St Petroc Minor – Padstow's is St Petroc Major. It's a 14th-century church that was almost entirely rebuilt in the 19th century, and a Grade I listed building. Unfortunately it was locked as it was very early still, and we felt we couldn't really knock on people's doors for a key, so we walked around it and tried to peer in the windows. Nothing doing, so we walked on. We chatted about the *endless prayers* that I read about in the papers on Petroc, which apparently he said while standing in the freezing river! Legends say that he used to pray for hours standing waist deep in the cold waters of Little Petherick Creek, reciting his psalter, to enhance the whole experience of his prayers. I didn't feel the need to emulate this at all.

The bridge by the church took us to the east of the creek, and we walked on through grassed fields and undulating hills to the hamlet of Mellingey, which means 'mill house'. We had been looking out for an ancient settlement, marked on the map, that was supposed to be near here but, by the time we had refreshed ourselves with a cup of tea sitting on a sharp corner on a small lane, we forgot. It was only about twenty minutes later that I realised where we had in fact been sitting, and by that time it was too far to go back. The settlement had been, we worked out, just behind us as we had sat drinking our tea! A few rubble stones in the field had been missed. We had actually thought a mound near Blable House was the settlement, but it turned out to be a manure heap instead.

However, Blable was also an ancient settlement originally. According to the brilliant publication from Pelican Studios on the Saints' Way, the name derives from the word meaning 'wolf pit' – *blyth-poll*. Wolves were once very common throughout Britain, so Blable was where they trapped wolves. They were so numerous that King Edgar, in the 10th century, demanded three hundred wolfskins as a tribute from King Constantine of Wales, probably because the pelts made lovely coats as well as hunting providing a means of culling. Petroc's pet wolf may not have been so out of place after all, except of course that it was tame.

The morning wore on and the fields were full of busy farmers trundling about on huge tractors. Unfortunately for us, they were all muck-spreading, laying down a thin film of slurry to fertilise their fields. It was terribly smelly walking across those fields. We tried holding our breath, but that wasn't very successful. Not long after Blable, we began the long gradient up to St Breock Downs and the highest point of the Way at 216 metres. The fields, besides being smelly, were rather soft underfoot and in places very soggy, so when we got onto a rough path, it was a relief. We started to near the enormous wind turbines of the St Breock Wind Farm that is still under construction. There were two base columns standing, as yet without their blades, and from a distance they resembled, in my imagination, docking ports for UFOs. The higher we got, the cooler it became. The wind wasn't strong, but it had a cold edge to it and we wanted to find shelter for a break.

We arrived at the top of the downs at the standing stone – the Longstone next to the Beacon – and sat with our backs to the stone and ate our sandwiches and had our hot tea. The prehistoric Bronze Age standing stone, or menhir, is reputed to weigh about 16.5 tonnes and stands just under five metres tall, and it tilts at a heart-stopping slant. No one knows the reason behind the various standing stones that can be found in Britain and in France, but it is suggested they could have marked the graves of important people, or served as meeting places. This particular menhir has also been called Men Gurta – 'stone of waiting';

a place for people to gather for a talk. It is still the focus of an annual get-together of local people. On the 4th of June every year, St Petroc's Day, the clergy and the people of the parishes he founded, Bodmin, Padstow and Little Petherick, meet for a service of commemoration to their patron saint. Despite the stone's alarming slant it continued to stand for the duration of our lunch, but it was a short stop as the cold and wind were becoming uncomfortable.

People walking the route many centuries before us probably wouldn't have noticed the cold wind or even the stink of muck-spreading. They were, I'm sure, a far tougher lot than us. The Saints' Way is also called the Drovers' Way or the Mariners' Way. Everyone coming down from Ireland or Wales by sea would be wary of going around the tip of Cornwall and those treacherous rocks at Land's End. Instead the short route from the north coast, from the mouth of the River Camel, to the River Fowey on the south coast, was far easier. In times past, the Camel and Fowey were considerably more navigable than today. It was but a four-mile stretch between them. Over the centuries the rivers have silted up, so now the gap is more like thirty miles. The route would have been used to transport cattle and trading goods as well as the odd saint or pilgrim. Gold was mined in Ireland, and it is possible that it was brought through here on its way to the Continent. Cornwall's richness in natural resources, such as tin and copper, was famous across the Old World. More evidence is being found all the time of centuries of trading, as far back as the Phoenicians and the Egyptians. Herodotus, the great traveller of the 5th century, mentions the Cassiterides – the Tin Islands – that could conceivably have been Britain. Cornwall is also rich with religious references – according to a local legend Joseph of Arimathea brought Jesus on one of his trading trips. It is William Blake's poem *Milton*, with its line *And did those feet in ancient times…* that makes us think of Cornwall's past. It is a long way to Glastonbury, where Joseph supposedly planted the flaming thorn bush, but ancient traders did travel far and wide, so why not?

Bodmin Moor was a much wilder place in the past than it is now, intersected as it is by roads and railways. When pilgrims walked across Cornwall to Brittany and further, they probably didn't walk the particular path we now know as the Saints' Way. Further onto the moor, in what would have been a very remote location, is a tiny hamlet. It is the site of an ancient, very small church dedicated to St Catherine of Alexandria. The hamlet is known as Temple. It is thought the original church was built c. 1120 as a refuge for pilgrims, on land that was owned by the Knights Templar. This was a holy order that was formed in 1118 to protect pilgrims in the Holy Land. The knights themselves all came from noble families who often gifted land to the order, such as this place, perhaps. By 1308 the order became the focus of attention across the Continent and King Edward II suppressed the order in England. From then on all of the properties then fell under the jurisdiction of the Knights Hospitallers Order instead. They were another order of military monks created to protect travelling pilgrims in the Holy Land.

St Catherine's continued to function as a church and refuge until the Reformation. It became infamous in the 16th century, as marriages were performed with neither banns nor licences, and suicides were buried there too. At this time suicides were denied burial in consecrated ground and were usually buried at crossroads. This was to confuse the dead when they tried to enter Heaven – they wouldn't know which direction to turn. Eventually all this was stamped out and the church and the building fell into disuse and eventually ruined. It got so bad that a century or so later, a tramp making use of it as a shelter was killed by the roof falling in. It was rebuilt in the middle of the 19th century and is now a little church tucked away amongst the greenery.

We were cold to the core, by the time we left the shelter of the standing stone and walking further along the downs, we saw another stone in a field. To us it looked far less impressive than the Longstone, and even the sheep surrounding it seemed to ignore it as they grazed away, except for one. On one of the tumuli surrounding the stone, a single sheep stood looking down its nose at us as we passed by. We wondered what it could possibly be thinking about. Keeping an eye on the sheep, we snuggled into our jackets to get warm and soon we were dropping down off the height of the downs and immediately the temperature rose – only by the tiniest bit, but it was enough. Here the track takes one down roads passing Hustyns resort and leisure club, and more tumuli and green fields full of yet more sheep. The day was beginning to draw to a close and the starlings were gathering on the telegraph wires. There were hundreds of them. Every now and again, for no obvious reason, they would suddenly take off and swoop around before landing again. As we got closer they became jumpy, and right above our heads, they soared away and disappeared. It was a glorious display.

We arrived at our night's rest – a B&B in the middle of what seemed to be nowhere – where we had a lovely welcome and a hearty supper. Unlike the Pilgrims' Way in Surrey and Kent, here there was almost no monastic infrastructure for pilgrims, excepting the Templars of course – no others that have survived, to our knowledge at least. I lay at night in my bed thinking of pilgrims of old huddled cold over an open fire, afraid of the wild wolves, and wishing for morning and daylight. I was warm and cosy in my comfy bed.

Daylight, when it arrived, brought more heavy, overcast skies, but no rain. We were deep in hilly country – steep valleys and sharp-sloped fields. We had to cross the Ruthern River almost immediately. 'Ruthern' means 'red' – the tin mining upstream would have stained the water red. The ford was about half a metre deep, but next to it was a bridge so we could stay dry. All around us here were snowdrops – whole dells of fragile-looking white-belled flowers. The trees were still bare, but the precursors of spring were very much in flower.

Our first stop in our second day was in the tiny village of Withiel up at the top of the next steep slope. It has a fine selection of 18th-century granite houses, all quite grand, and in the middle is the church. It is dedicated to Clement I, the third successor to St Peter as Bishop of Rome and pope (92–101). Clement himself had an unfortunate end. He fell foul of the Emperor Trajan's temper, who ordered his death. He was chained to an anchor and thrown into the sea, and as a result is now the patron saint of seafarers. The medieval church lists rectors all the way back to before 1297, but its most noted is the Prior Thomas Vyvyan who rebuilt the church in 1523 after it had fallen into ruin. The village was very quiet but for a woman on a horse, who trotted by wishing us a friendly good morning as we walked through the village looking for the next waymarker. Up and down fields, soft going but not too muddy, and every time weren't sure of our way we looked for one sure sign. The granite-and-slate stiles of Cornwall seemed as though they'd been there for time immemorial, and sometimes they were really quite high. Stepping up on the granite stones and climbing over the slate upright was tricky with a heavy backpack on if you lost your balance, as happened to me once, but luckily I managed to right myself in time. Passing by the oddly named place of Lanzota, we tried to imagine a Celtic settlement here. *Lan* is Cornish for 'church site' and *Zota* is thought to be the name of a saint. Now the moles have taken up residence and the fields are covered in simply hundreds of molehills, giving it the impression of a huge mole city.

Soon we walked by the tiny hamlet of Retire and into Tremore. This was very manicured, the lawns trimmed precisely and the flower beds neat and pretty. It was most out of keeping with the rest of the countryside, but as we climbed out of the hamlet the landscape changed back to large vistas and open fields. We stopped briefly to admire Tremore House and the Celtic cross lying on the grass at the crossroads before walking on, down deserted roads and a couple of fields, towards the village of Lanivet. We had hoped to have lunch here, but we'd walked far too quickly and were too early. Nonetheless we popped into the local shop, bought pasties and carried them with us. Lanivet sits in a very deep little valley. The road down was hard on the knees, but not so much as the road on the other side coming out again. At a junction in the village, I realised Lanivet is just about the middle distance of the Saints' Way. The name is derived from *Lan* (church site) and *Vet* (a pagan sacred grove). That suggests this is a very old sacred place, and it grew into an important settlement. The church was all locked up, so we simply wandered the graveyard. It was full of huge, ancient yews and several time-worn stone crosses. One features an odd figure of a man with a tail. The oldest belongs to a hogback grave that is said to date from Viking times. The village, and especially the church itself, is said to mark the exact centre of Cornwall too.

Now we were on the second stage of the Saints' Way and we found many more Celtic crosses going south. They point out the way between the parishes of Lanivet and the next village of size, Lanlivery. We climbed out of the valley and found ourselves walking down the side of the incredibly noisy A30 – perhaps the most important road in Cornwall. After the quiet of the valleys it was hard to bear, but we had no option. Less than a kilometre along this road we passed by the modern farm at St Ingunger. This had been a very important Christian site and the home of a hermit named St Congar of Congresbury in the 6th century. There was a holy well and a chapel, and eventually a large monastery. Now it has extensive modern farming sheds and barns, plus offices, and even the South West School of Photography. The cross here is a wheel-headed wayside cross standing next to the Saints' Way marker, showing us the route up to Fenton Pits and more crosses. It was freezing by now and we looked for somewhere to shelter and eat our (by now cold) pasties and drink hot tea to warm us up. We crouched in the corner of a bend next to a house that gave us some shelter from the cold, which surprised drivers as they shot down the narrow road.

Heads down after lunch and keeping on the road, we walked almost directly south and saw in front of us the great height of Helman Tor. It stands at 209 metres, not quite as high as St Breock Downs, but this being a tor, it is rugged and rocky by its very nature. It is the most northern edge of a granite ridge and is surrounded by marshy wetlands. The hummocks and hollows of the surrounding fields show evidence of tin smelting in the past, and now the area is a nature reserve and the home to many birds. I think we saw skylarks, but everything else had been chased away as the tor was being worked on. There were men in bright orange jackets crawling over the rocks and setting fire to the surrounding dead vegetation, mainly bracken, in preparation for the arrival of spring. It was such a pity we couldn't go up to the top. Within the tor are the remains of a six-thousand-year-old Neolithic settlement and something called a logan stone. A logan or rocking stone is a geological term to describe a stone that has weathered to the point of being so well balanced that it can be rocked on its surrounding stone base by one person. Because of their strangeness they used to be regarded as being mystical. They are peculiar to tors and mostly in the south-west of Britain. There aren't many in the country and it would have been interesting to see one, but instead we had to walk on by, while the men in orange carried on with their controlled burning.

The path wound around the waist of the tor and carried on along the granite ridge in a more-or-less straight line. This is clearly an ancient path as it was the highest and driest land to walk on. A high hedge encloses it and it is just wide enough for a narrow vehicle. Walking here was a mixed blessing as the enclosing hedges did screen out the wind, but they also obscured the view so, despite being on a high ridge, we saw little until we came to a gate and, glancing over, saw a magnificent vista off to the west, with the sea glinting in the very far distance. The path soon widened and as we rounded a bend we saw a sight that must have gladden the heart of any pilgrim – a church and refuge.

A refuge for the pilgrims and our night's stop too, and we walked on down delightful small roads, dodging the cars coming home from their working day. Before long we arrived at the foot of the church. Lanlivery's church is dedicated to St Brevita or Bryvyth. Everywhere I have researched has said one thing about St Brevita – of her there is absolutely nothing known. I imagine her name has been changed or abbreviated. Earlier histories suggest the village itself was dedicated to or called after another obscure holy man called St Vorck. That would sound like *Lan-le-Vorck* (church site of St Vorck), and with common usage could have become Lanlivery.

The 15th-century granite tower is peculiarly tall, up to thirty metres. Its south-facing wall was whitewashed and used as a landmark for ships out at sea coming into Fowey Harbour. The church itself was originally erected in the 12th century, but was added to in the 15th century and extensively restored in the 19th. Hidden behind a screen in the north chapel, we found a fine alabaster bas-relief of a praying man before the crucifix. Sir John Betjeman, in his *Collins Pocket Guide to English Parish Churches: The South*, described the church as *one of the great churches of Cornwall*. A painted wooden plaque hangs on the wall of the bell tower, written on the orders of King Charles I to the people of Lanlivery in thanks for the support they gave during the Civil War. Across from the church is the 12th-century Crown Inn that was built to house the original builders of the church and has stood ever since. It's a fantastic medieval longhouse converted into a very homely inn with small nooks and crannies, and we had a lovely night's rest and supper sitting near its huge roaring fire. We could have stayed for days.

As we woke the following day, our last on the Saints' Way, the wind was blowing and the rain was pounding on the roof and against the windows of our room. It was dark, and not a welcome for the day. Luckily by breakfast time the rain had passed over and the sun started peeping out. Glorious morning.

All full of breakfast and sad to leave the Crown, we grabbed our stuff and walked off, visiting the church one more time. A quick walk around and we were off through the graveyard and into the hills. The sun shone brilliantly and all the clouds simply melted away, giving us clear blue skies as we headed away from Lanlivery. We passed one more standing stone in the garden of a house and headed off across fields to a place called No Man's Land. We had to rejoin the road which took us down to the A390, which turned out to be another fast and noisy stretch of road – the main artery to Plymouth and very busy. The route took us about five hundred metres down before we could turn off up a small lane into the yard of a muddy farm. The cows looked at us with great interest – it was obviously near enough feeding time and they must have thought we were very mean not giving them anything.

By now we were not far off the River Fowey, walking parallel to it. This stretch was all on small, just-about-deserted roads, and the occasional car forced us to lean into the hedge. The rain started again and then the sun, and we trudged on down and up the road, until a small waymarker told us to go sharp left – and immediately into a field with several horses. There were lots of different types: a huge shire horse, a fine-boned riding horse and a Shetland pony amongst them. They completely ignored us as we climbed the hill through their field, and as we took a rest at the top to enjoy the superb view.

As delightful as the view was in the sunshine, the heavy black clouds raced overhead and within moments released inches of torrential rain. We threw on our hoods again and hurried on, over a field of swedes very close to harvest, over a rickety stile and skirted a field of bright new grass. Finally we reached the village of Golant, and it was really raining hard. The church of Petroc's friend, St Samson, was tucked away, sitting very prettily in amongst the camellias flowering bright red in the graveyard. We ran for it. In my haste I failed to open the gate, so we climbed over it (it was quite low) and dashed for the porch and into the church, clanging open the heavy wooden door. Oh, what a delight this place was. It truly felt like a sanctuary, not only from the belting rain, but in spirit too. It had a small sort of 'kitcheny' area at the back, so we stripped off our wet gear and let it drip onto the stone floor while we sighed with pleasure at being out of the wet and looked around. The church is barrel-roofed and, like so many of the Cornish churches, has an enormous free-standing organ. It had been redecorated quite recently, with everything very white and very clean, and a skylight must have been added too, as it was lovely and bright. All the pews had beautifully made colourful kneelers depicting all sorts of subjects from flowers to crosses. It felt very welcoming indeed. It was built, according to the local website, in the 14th century but it has a far longer history behind it.

St Samson of Dol, to whom it is dedicated, is a very important saint amongst the great horde in Cornwall and many regard him as the greatest missionary to ever come out of Britain. He was one of the first to welcome Petroc to Cornwall. Samson was born c. 485 to noble parents, Amon of Demetia and Anna of Gwent. His life is recorded in the *Vita Sancti Samsonis*, written sometime between 610 and 820. A prophecy at his birth led his parents to place him immediately in the care of St Illtud at Llantwit. The story goes that Samson later left Llantwit, either because he desired a greater austerity, or else because the jealous nephews of St Illtud tried to kill him, so he moved to Caldey Island off the Welsh coast. Eventually he became abbot of Caldey Abbey after the last abbot, St Pyr, killed himself by falling drunk into a well. As with many devout men Samson went to study in Ireland, and soon became famous for his miracles. On his return he lived as a sort of hermit with his father and a couple of others, before moving on to Cornwall where was consecrated bishop by Dubricius in about 521. He worked in Cornwall as a missionary founding monasteries and churches, as at Golant. Finally he moved to Armorica (Brittany) after he was warned by an angel to leave England, and landed on the coast near Dol. Under his spiritual guidance, Dol became an important holy centre. He founded many other monasteries and abbeys in Brittany as well as in the Scilly Isles and Guernsey. The king subsequently nominated him as Bishop of Dol. Samson lived until he was eighty-five and was buried at Dol. Such was his importance that King Æthelstan of Wessex (924–939) acquired a couple of relics of St Samson, his arm and his crozier, which he kept at his monastery at Milton Abbas.

Samson is often depicted holding either a staff or a cross with a dove and holding a book, but in the window of his church he is standing on the slain dragon. The story of the dragon comes from one of Samson's missionary travels. In the hundred of Trigg (hundreds were administrative centres), he came across a pagan idol being worshipped by a chieftain called Gwythian. When a young boy of his tribe was killed in a race by a broken neck, Samson said that if the chieftain and his people ceased worshipping pagan idols and started believing in the True God, then he, through the power of God, would bring the boy back to life. They agreed, and Samson prayed over the boy until he was alive and well. The chieftain then asked if Samson would rid him of a terrible dragon. Samson entered its lair, which was in a cave nearby, and slew the beast. Thus he built the church on the spot at Golant. Supposedly, and coincidentally, there is a cave near the Iron Age site of Castle Dore a few miles distant which fits the bill. This ancient site saw the surrender of the Parliamentarian Army to Charles I in 1644, when it was used as the army's camp. The king apparently slept in his carriage at Golant before this surrender, which was his army's greatest success before its final crushing defeat.

This is not the only story attached to St Samson's Church. It is said that the most famous of Cornwall's kings (or Kernow as Cornwall was then called), King Mark and his beloved but faithless wife Iseult, would have worshipped in a church on this site. This doomed love story is thought to come from the Arthurian legends and maybe really refers to

Lancelot and Guinevere. In this version Mark sent his adored nephew Tristan to collect his Irish bride, the Princess Iseult. On the journey back they both drank a magic potion that caused them to fall in love. Iseult married Mark, whom she also loved, but she was obsessed by Tristan, whom she continued to meet clandestinely whenever possible. Mark eventually found out and Tristan was imprisoned, but he soon escaped, taking Iseult with him. After a while the magic potion wore off and, although still madly in love, Tristan vowed to King Mark that he, Tristan, would leave the country, never to return, so Iseult and Mark could be happy together. Mark and Iseult went in gratitude to the church at Golant to say thanks. However, the king's barons demanded the queen undergo an Ordeal to prove her fidelity. Iseult agreed, but said it had to be at a place called Blancheland, which could only be reached by crossing a marsh. She sent word to Tristan to dress as a leper and go to the marsh at Blancheland. When the party of nobles and the king arrived there to observe the ordeal, the disguised Tristan sent them the wrong way, but when Iseult arrived she asked him to carry her on his back over the marsh. By doing this she could truthfully say, at her trial later, that no man had ever been between her legs other than the king and the leper who had carried her across the marsh.

The end of their story is one of more double-crossing. Tristan fled to France, where he married another woman called Iseult. When he was dying he sent a message begging for his first love to come and nurse him. He told the sailors delivering the message to hoist black sails on their return if she would not come. His second wife overheard this and, full of jealousy, told him that the ships had returned with black sails. He died alone and his beloved Iseult died soon after of a broken heart – perhaps their great love had brought them together after all, in death. So this, perhaps the greatest legend of Cornwall and the subject of one of Wagner's great operas, is centred on this wonderful church.

We wandered about for ages, looking at the detail and enjoying the serenity. The present rector, from a long list begun by Richard Baker in

1528, has tried to make all visits as pleasurable as possible, and they have for sale, tucked at the back of the church, small mementos for one to take home. While I was poking about I noticed my sister buying a mug to add to the weight of her backpack.

But it was time to move on, so with the rain still falling and obscuring the view, making us keep our heads low, we walked off through the village and onto the final leg of the Saints' Way. The path between the two villages of Golant and Fowey is still very well used, both by locals and as part of the walking trails around here. On a clear and dry day, it must be a truly magical walk through the woods. The views to our left overlooking the river were utterly gorgeous, but would have been even better if they had been clear rather than through the hazing rain. Still, it was lovely. The trees created an avenue over our heads. The path took us along the side of the Fowey and down to the most wonderful creek, and then up the other side and the last slow decline into the town and the port.

Reaching the edge of Fowey itself we found ourselves walking in between houses on very narrow lanes instead of through woods and open fields. Cars coming down the road forced us onto the front doorsteps of the houses to let them pass, such was the narrowness. These medieval lanes curled up and around the houses and we followed them to the end of the Saints' Way and the church of the Irish St Finbarr. We had arrived, but I wanted to see one more thing. We walked down to the water's edge and looked across the harbour. Punches Cross is a white cross on the rocks on the eastern side of the harbour, and legend says it is the landing site of Jesus and his uncle Joseph of Arimathea, when they came to trade. The name 'Punches' is supposed to be a corruption of 'Pontius', as it seems Pontius Pilate also made it to these parts and landed on these rocks too.

It was the end of our walk, but for the pilgrims this was not the end of theirs. For them this was the beginning of the greatest test of their faith and abilities. Now of course they had to find a ship to take them on to the great shrines of St James at Santiago de Compostela, or Rome or even perhaps to the Holy Land too. This was truly the beginning and not the end for them. For us it was to the pub for lunch and then a lift home, completely happy and most content.

3

St Augustine:
A Reluctant Missionary

Kent
6th century
Twenty-five kilometres
Map: OS Explorer 150

S t Augustine did not want to come to Britain. He was happy in Rome. He was ordered to go by the pope, but even so he turned back after a few kilometres just to ask again – did he really have to go? Yes, said the pope.

The pope in question was Pope Gregory the Great who, the story goes, had been rather taken by some pretty children in the marketplace in Rome. Sometime in the 580s, before he became pope, he was walking by a slave auction when he spotted two golden-haired children, and he asked where these 'angels' had come from. He was told they were 'Angles' and they had come from Deira in Britain. It is said he then made the decision that it was time to bring God to the Angles, and hence his commands to Augustine to carry the Christian message to the far reaches of the known world.

In 596 Augustine was the prior of the Monastery of St Andrew on the Caelian Hill in Rome. Although he was reportedly content with his position at St Andrew's, Pope Gregory I chose him as the leader of an extraordinary mission. Augustine was not happy about it and argued that he was too pathetic and lacking in ability for such a role, but the pope thought otherwise. Gregory was a man of huge ambition and he was determined to evangelise the Anglo-Saxon pagans of England. He had wanted to go himself and had in fact set off some years previously, but the citizens of Rome had demonstrated with such horror at the prospect of losing their deacon that the then-pope ordered his return. Gregory became pope himself in 590, and soon after decided to send a mission in his name. Parts of England had been Christianised already during the time of the Romans, but as they left the invading hordes of Vikings and Anglo-Saxons came rolling over in waves, bringing their own gods with them, and Christianity had been pushed to the furthermost extremes of the island. Gregory aimed to re-evangelise the land. His chronicles suggest he had heard that a mission would be favourably received. Perhaps that suggestion came from the court of the King of Kent, who had recently married a Frankish Princess from Paris. Bertha, the daughter of the King of the Franks, was a Christian and had in her marriage promises been allowed to keep her religion and have her chaplain with her. There have been suggestions too that the queen had urged her husband to write to the pope and invite missionaries to his kingdom. Whatever the truth of so long ago, Gregory deemed that England was ripe for the God of Rome.

Augustine had no choice, and he was sent off with thirty or forty fellow monks on the long, arduous and dangerous trip to England. The closer he got, the more horror stories he heard. He was told of terrible torture and mutilations, and how barbaric the people were. In fright he and his brothers headed back to Rome. Gregory refused to listen to them and sent them off again – go and evangelise. So on they went and reached the coast of France, and took ship to arrive on the Isle of Thanet at Ebbsfleet. Only one hundred or so years earlier, a more formidable and deadly arrival had found the bay at Ebbsfleet: a mercenary band of Angle, Saxon and Northmen warriors led by two brothers, Hengist and Horsa. They had been invited over by King Vortigern of Kent to quell a quarrelsome neighbour dispute. They quickly sorted that out, but then told Vortigern that they now held the land. It had been a strategic mistake, and from then on the pagan Hengist has been known as the father of the Kings of Kent. So now, only a mere hundred years later, another, altogether different invasion was beginning.

St Augustine and his band of brothers, having landed and gazed about them in fear, sent some emissaries to the court of King Æthelberht, descendant of Hengist, in Canterbury to ask permission to land and meet him. Æthelberht ordered that Augustine and his people should remain on the Isle of Thanet, which at that time was truly an island. It was some days later, according to the Venerable Bede, that the king agreed to meet with the men from Rome. But he and his people were all afraid of the Roman magic that they had heard rumours of, so Æthelberht and his priests met Augustine's mission under an oak tree, out in the open where any magic would not work. The oak was sacred to the pagans and hence would protect them. The website archbishopofcanterbury. org includes a quote of Æthelberht's stating that even though he wasn't going to fall under the Romans' spell and "forsake what I have so long believed", he decided to allow Augustine to come and preach amongst his people, in the hope of creating converts, in Canterbury. Augustine had arrived.

The first thing we saw when we got to the small village of Ebbsfleet where Augustine landed was the enormous Viking longship called

Hugin. It was quite impressive knowing that it had been built exactly as the longships of the Viking times were, and that it was no toy, having been rowed all the way from Denmark in 1949 to commemorate the 1,500 years since the first landing on English shores. I didn't think its yellow-headed dragon was right, though – I felt it should have been a deep blood red. But Viking longships weren't the point of us being here, so having got the gist of where Augustine would have landed had he been coming today, we walked slightly inland to where he did supposedly land. Of course we don't know a definitive place, but in 1884 the 2nd Earl Granville erected a magnificent cross at a point considered to be the spot. Known as St Augustine's Cross, it stands on an inconspicuous bend on a very minor road – so easily missed and just standing in a field; no fanfare. It was the true start of the walk following a route that St Augustine and his brothers probably would have walked to Canterbury. It was a lovely sunny day, early spring and the trees were bright with new green growth – that special green which dulls and deepens as the summer progresses, but now was sparkling with life.

In times past Thanet was very much an island, separated from the mainland by the Wantsum Channel. It had been wide enough for ships to sail between the isle and the mainland right up until 1672. Since then silt has all but closed the channel up, and now Thanet is an island in name only. There are a large number of channels throughout this low-lying area still, but they are mostly man-made, created by the monks over the centuries to create fields and fish ponds. It is very flat and easy walking, which gave my companion (my sister again) and me time to listen to the birds in between the trains passing next to us as we walked. After we'd walked away from Augustine's Cross we followed a footpath by the side of the railway directly west towards the town of Minster. After only a few miles, we veered away from the tracks and made our way through fields being ploughed in readiness for new crops. Ahead of us the spire of Minster's church peeked out from above the trees on the small hill. Minster had been at one time an important port when the Wantsum was navigable. Now it's a small village, dominated by its abbey and the church dedicated to St Mary. Every time I walk towards a church spire it puts me right into the footsteps of pilgrims from the past; it invites one in.

The abbey is a little more discreet than the church's spire. It is a working convent, or more formally a conventual priory. It houses thirteen Benedictine nuns who are the heart of a community with an enormous heritage. In 670 the brothers of the Mercian King's wife, Ermenburga, were murdered by the King of Kent. (Ermenburga was the great-granddaughter of King Æthelberht himself.) Rather than being paid blood money in recompense she asked for land to set up a 'house of prayer'. The king was eager to grant that, and Ermenburga sent her pet deer to wander freely, and all land the deer encompassed became hers. The deer is now the emblem of Minster, and images of the many saints attached to Minster Abbey depict a deer. Ermenburga changed her name and became St Domneva. Her daughter was abbess for thirty years following Domneva's death, before she too was canonised and became St Mildred. Many miracles of healing were attributed to Mildred after her death. Eadburga became the third abbess in 725, and she and her sister nuns were very supportive of St Boniface and other missionaries working on the Continent. They sent manuscripts, and their correspondence attests to the help they gave. The abbey's geographical position made it most valuable as a bridge to the Continent, but it also made it vulnerable to the various invasions of Vikings and Normans. However, it survived pretty much intact until Henry VIII's heavy hand fell upon it. Some of the buildings were torn down and others were simply allowed to fall into ruin until 1602 when King James I gave away the lands. The abbey remained in private hands, changing owners every now and again, until 1937 when the then-owners decided to sell up and find something smaller. They weren't successful, but a local priest was struck by the idea of the building being restored to monastic use, so he wrote letters to every monastic house in England asking if any wanted to take it on. He too was unsuccessful, so he turned to the Continent. The day his letter arrived in the Benedictine House of St Walburga in Eichstätt, Bavaria was the same day that the Nazi authorities had informed the abbess that part of her convent would be requisitioned. She saw it as a sign. It wasn't easy, but she managed to buy the property and send over a few nuns, and since then it has survived and grown.

The feeling as one walks in is one of absolute serenity and sanctity. A lot of the abbey is closed for most of the time, which is hardly surprising since it is the nuns' home, but the Chapel of Our Lady and St Andrew that was built after a fire in 1987 is open all the time. We did have the opportunity to simply wander around a bit in the garden, tended with such care by the sisters. The relics of St Mildred are still in situ, brought back from Canterbury when the abbey was refounded in 1937.

Mildred was a most beloved saint of medieval times – as important as St Augustine at one time, and King Cnut and his wife Queen Emma in the 11th century credited her with saving their lives when they were caught in a storm in the English Channel while returning from Rome. Her church in Canterbury is, I believe, the oldest one within the walls of the city, before the Norman Conquest in 1066.

Coming away from the abbey to the Church of St Mary the Virgin wasn't exactly a let-down, but to have two such magnificent places in a tiny spot is almost too much. So after a short stop we moved on to what would have been wetlands in the distant past. The horizon was huge, big-sky country; there is nothing to hinder one's view of the clouds and planes' contrails across the sky above. A lovely sight. The fields are bounded by channels and canals still full of water, and I read that most of the land was flooded the majority of the time for the fish industry. In medieval times, the bishops would instruct the monks of all the monasteries within their See to cultivate as many fish farms as possible. Monks always ate a lot of fish. The rules of St Benedict decreed that meat could only be eaten on certain days because of its connection to gluttony and lasciviousness, so instead fish was often on the menu. The fields now grow wheat and barley – barley especially, to feed the famous Kent breweries. Most of the earth had been recently turned over in preparation for new sowing. We walked along the sides of the great fields, next to the channels filled with weed-infested water. The frogs were croaking away and occasionally a fish would surface to gulp air before disappearing quickly below to safety.

We followed a public footpath that zigzagged across the flatlands, sticking to the field's edges, until we reached the Abbot's Wall. The Domesday Book of 1086 states that the Monastery of St Augustine in Canterbury owned this land near Minster, so all decisions and any produce belonged to them. The Abbot's Wall, and another one further away called the Monk's Wall, were built by the monks to enclose and reclaim land for agricultural use before the 13th century. Now the Abbot's Wall is just a bump in the field with yet another ditch next to it.

We crossed over to find our first waymarker – St Augustine's Way. It was ever so slightly confusing, with arrows pointing in all directions. After a certain amount of crawling through a bit of overgrown hedging, we found the right direction and headed off down to the River Stour. One needs to be careful, because finding yourself on the wrong side of one of these channels would lead to a lot of backtracking; there are very few bridges. The River Stour has always been of great importance to this area. It used to run into the Wantsum Channel, but since silting and reclamation it is now used for fishing (mainly pike, bream and roach), and recreation (especially lazing along in a small motorboat). It runs like a great, sluggish brown snake through the fields.

As we reached the riverbank we turned right, paralleling the Saxon Shore Way on the other bank. The Saxon Shore Way starts in Gravesend on the north coast of Kent and winds its way down to and across the landscape for 262 kilometres, to finish in Hastings. It looked to be a pretty well-trodden path, but on our side we could barely make out any sort of path at all. The nettles had taken over completely. What a nightmare. I had, in deference to the lovely sunshine, decided to wear shorts – oh, what a ghastly mistake. We were wading waist deep through them. For a few short stretches we were back walking on the edges of fields bordering the river with the nettles taking second place to crops, but then came more nettles. We continued along the river, watching the occasional boat amble up or down, until we came to Plucks Gutter. A wonderful pub is more or less the only sign of habitation in Plucks Gutter. It was a most welcome break with a lovely cooling lemonade, plus a comfy sit-down in the garden. There we were, pretty hot and sweaty, surrounded by cool-looking customers out for a day's lunch.

According to what I can find on the internet, Plucks Gutter was named after a Dutchman called Ploeg (meaning 'plough'), who may well have been here to plough a ditch in the marshland, i.e. drain it. Here the two rivers, the Little Stour and the Great Stour, joined the Wantsum Channel of yesteryear. Now the river is simply called the Stour River. It wasn't far from here that King Alfred scored a great victory over the Vikings, at a place called Blood Point. But there are no Vikings, nor smugglers (I think), around today. So onward and hugging the river still, but now on the south side, we had a glorious walk on a wide mown-grass path until it ran out and straight into the nettles again. This is the problem of walking in the spring. It's glorious to see the buds on the trees beginning to burst forth and plants practically growing before one's eyes, but it does mean that the nettles are at their most potent.

Now we were walking on the Saxon Shore Way, following the edges of the barren fields freshly turned for the summer crop, until we came to a sign off to the left pointing to the historic church of Stourmouth. The village is named, as it states, as the point where the River Stour entered the sea. But that was a long time ago. A sign in the village told us the area was most probably underwater in Roman times, but by King Alfred's time it was already draining, although still with enough water to pursue and destroy those ships of the Danes' fleet in the Wantsum Channel. Since then the sea has receded a considerable way, stranding the village in the midst of flat fields. The 1086 Domesday Book records Stourmouth, but the church is thought to be originally Anglo-Saxon. Of course it has been rebuilt over the centuries, but in 1979 it became redundant and was allowed to fall into disrepair. Now, though, it has been restored and its upkeep assured by the Redundant Churches Fund.

What a wonderful atmosphere it has. At first I thought we hadn't the chance to go in, as a forbidding sign on the door threatened dire consequences on entering, so we contented ourselves with wandering about the cemetery. This in itself was impressive, with many tilting headstones, so old and eroded it was impossible to read names and dates.

As we began to walk away a woman suddenly appeared with her dog and asked if we wanted to go inside. "Oh yes," we said, and she simply walked in – no key, no alarms, no fuss. Oh well, so much for taking notice of scary signs.

She smiled and said, "Just pull the door to when you leave." The church was lovely: very spartan and unelaborate – some carvings were in fact made from papier mâché so we were asked not to touch them. There were a few very old stained-glass windows, but its charm was in its atmosphere.

Stourmouth's church does open its doors at other times, though: it is possible to organise to sleep in the church – champing, it's called; camping in the church. I think it would be fine for a group, but I would feel distinctly uneasy sleeping alone there in the dark of the night. Coming out of the church again we retraced our footsteps back to our route for our night's stop in Canterbury with a bus from Upstreet.

Our start again from Upstreet took us past the Grove Ferry Inn with its pigs in the front garden, and then a quick right turn to walk down the proper path of the Stour Valley Walk by the side of the river. It was a gorgeous morning and we even put on sun cream to shield ourselves from the lovely rays. We were walking down the Stodmarsh National Nature Reserve – a birdwatching sanctuary. The area is full of reeds and wetlands and probably looks much the same as in medieval times. Then the monks would graze horses here as their manure made for great fertiliser for the crops. According to the reserve's leaflet it is particularly important for bittern (not sure if we saw one), marsh harrier (saw a bird of prey, so it's possible), the shining ramshorn snail (sadly not, but it is very rare), and water voles (yes!). The reserve is a couple of miles of paths, but as we walked out we climbed up high on the riverbank, with a brilliant view over it as it flows smoothly towards Canterbury and into superb bluebell woods. The conditions must be perfect for them because there were just acres of them shimmering in the sunlight between the trees.

I don't think it's been recorded anywhere what time of year Augustine and his brothers arrived in England. We don't know if he walked through dells of bluebells, or the withering heat of summer, or the freezing cold of winter. Æthelberht allowed Augustine to come to preach in Canterbury, and not long after Æthelberht himself became a Christian, baptised by Augustine before thousands more of his people, on Christmas Day in 597. A letter by Pope Gregory to the Patriarch of Alexandria in June 598 says that Augustine had baptised ten thousand Christians. Perhaps a slight exaggeration, but still there must have been a lot. So the beginning of Augustine's mission was so far a success. According to Bede, he then sent his brother monk Laurence back to Rome to report on the success and to ask lots of questions for guidance. We have a lot of detail from these letters of what Augustine needed to know to set up a church/monastery, as well as the fears that he obviously felt regarding his fitness for the undertaking. Initially it is recorded that he preached at St Martin's Church that the king had built for the queen, but subsequently he founded the Monastery of Saints Peter and Paul on the land outside the city walls, given by the king. That monastery is now the ruin of St Augustine's Abbey, Canterbury.

But it was only the early days of Christianising England. First he needed to be a bishop. Bede states that Augustine was consecrated such in Arles by Bishop Aetherius, but when is not clear, and is still a point of debate amongst the experts. In 601 more missionaries arrived from Rome, bringing with them new orders from the pope for Augustine to follow through. The pope instructed Augustine to ordain twelve suffragan bishops, and send one of them to York to set up a new episcopal centre there. The pope's idea had been always to have two metropolitans (episcopal centres) in England, one in York to convert the northern half of the country, and one in London. He had intended the archbishop metropolitan to move from Canterbury to London, but that may not have happened because London was within the sub-kingdom of a nephew of King Æthelberht's who was a pagan and did not wish to convert; hence it stayed in Canterbury.

Only eight years after Augustine's arrival at Ebbsfleet, he died in Canterbury and was buried in the portico of his abbey. It was after the Normans' arrival in 1066 that the site became a huge pilgrimage centre, and then his remains were housed in a shrine in the centre of the church, flanked by those of Laurence, his successor to the See of Canterbury, and of Justus, whom Augustine had consecrated as the Bishop of Rochester. Miracles attributed to him came only later when the chronicler Goscelin wrote his hagiography in 1090, and probably made up an awful lot of it. However, that is not to say that Augustine's role in bringing Christianity to England was not enormous. The earlier Celtic Christians had not tried to convert the heathen Anglo-Saxons and Viking pagans, and had stayed in their corner of the country, but Augustine, directed by the ambitious Gregory, saw the whole country as part of God's plan.

As we walked down into Canterbury we headed not towards the centre of town and the spectacular cathedral in the heart of the crowded city, but a little to the east, outside of the walls. We carried on down, paralleling the Stour, but remained high on the hill, staying on the

Stour Valley Walk, until past Fordwich we veered left, south, through Chequers Wood and over Scotland Hills, skirting the golf course to come down onto the Roman road where we turned right towards the city. Here the road took us directly to the quiet ruins of Augustine's abbey, almost ignored by the vast crowds drawn by St Thomas Becket and the cathedral. Augustine's splendid shrine was destroyed during the Henry Reformation, but his gravesite is still within the heart of the church that he founded all those centuries ago.

4

St Cuthbert's World

Northumbria
7th century
One hundred kilometres
Maps: Explorer 338, OL16, 340, and
Harvey: Scotland's Great Trails: XT40

St Cuthbert, both the man and the legend, was hard to find as I walked his Way from Melrose to the Holy Island, also called Lindisfarne. I tried to find him but he was elusive; he hid behind the countryside. Perhaps in hindsight, he wanted me to appreciate the beauty of the land, and not be aware of its story through his own. Perhaps he was so humble he didn't really feel as though he measured up to what I could see before my eyes. Perhaps, or perhaps it was simply my imagination... whatever, but it didn't get in the way of a wonderful walk.

Whichever it was – beauty or humility – the Way was amazing. A hundred kilometres across the Scottish Borders, crossing into England high across the Cheviot Hills, into the Northumberland National Park and on to the coast, and a spit of land that twice a day becomes a refuge from the secularism of the mainland; to relax into the calm atmosphere of a small and welcoming community.

This is now one of the foremost walks in northern Britain and I was longing to do it. But I was wary of poor weather. I read the route is often high and exposed and could be very cold. I don't like being cold: it makes for shivery rest stops and too many clothes. I waited and waited in the spring for the weather to get warmer, but storm after storm was blowing across northern Britain. While the south, where I was, basked in ever-growing sunshine and warmth as the sun climbed higher, it seemed to be missing Northumberland. I couldn't wait forever. I had to simply go and live with it, whatever was thrown at me. I knew I wouldn't be sleeping rough or in campsites – brrr, no way. All the guides and everything I read about the route recommended booking lodgings in advance, and I was glad I did when I found out how small some of the places were; one had precisely two and a half beds, the half being a child's bed. So, with all booked and the train organised, I packed my backpack and travelled north.

Train journeys are so brilliant. I love watching the land slip by, changing here and there from meadow to hillside and from farm to village to town. We slid into York, where a friend, who had agreed to share this adventure with me, joined me. We chatted about kit and boots and backpacks and what fun it all was. She has done a lot of walking and we swapped stories as we raced north. In a few hours we reached Berwick-upon-Tweed. The station has two platforms – one going north and the other going south – and trains thunder through to all parts of Britain, from the furthest south-west and Penzance, to the northernmost reaches of Scotland. We found the bus stop and waited a short while for the bus to Melrose. With a few passengers on board, our driver shot off into the countryside. I made sure I watched where we were going as the bus slewed around corners and sent us passengers swinging from the poles, even though we were sitting down. Every now and again a raucous bell signalled a passenger wanted to get off this roller-coaster ride. At one stop a frail, elderly, smartly dressed smiling woman made her way to the front of the bus where the driver had emerged from his protective box. He gently helped her off, not only down the steps of the bus, but across the road too, onto the pavement and watched briefly as she started to make her way towards the collection of houses in her village. Then we were off again, at a fast pace, and before long we reached Melrose's market square.

I was delighted – the sun was shining, cool though it was, and Melrose looked lovely. The town has two main streets, and our first night's B&B was on one of them, Buccleuch Street, which has at its end the reason for the town in the first place, namely Melrose Abbey. We found our lodgings after a small wander around town, not only in search of our B&B but somewhere to eat too. We were spoilt for choice with four possible pubs, all of which looked fine from the outside. Settled and without our packs, we headed off to the abbey. A wedding was in progress, so we slowly mused around the outside of the abbey church, in amongst the ruined stones of the monks' quarters and their living areas, from the kitchens to the cloister and even their latrines. Melrose is described as being one of the four great abbeys of the Scottish Borders; King David I of Scotland founded it in 1136. Over the years, with all the Border Wars and Reiver raids between the Scots and the English, the abbey has been destroyed and rebuilt several times. What we were looking at – according to the very good information boards scattered about the grounds – is 15th- and 16th-century repairs and 19th-century restorations. The abbey is very proud of its humorous carvings. I found the pig playing bagpipes but I couldn't find the fat monk, nor the cook with a ladle. Such whimsy. I wonder if the abbot really knew what he had on the high walls of his abbey.

Melrose housed the Cistercians who came up from Rievaulx Abbey in Yorkshire. The abbey itself was finally destroyed during what's known as the Rough Wooing in 1544, when King Henry VIII wanted to marry the baby Mary, Queen of Scots to his son Edward. He thought he'd win over the Scots by destroying the Border abbeys and devastating the countryside. It was thankfully saved in the early 19th century by the then-Duke of Buccleuch, who subsequently gave it to Historic Scotland – probably because the embalmed heart of Robert the Bruce is buried here, and King Alexander II too, who died in 1249.

Soon the wedding was over, so we walked in, down the nave and over to where the high altar would have been, to a table covered with a white tablecloth and decorated with pretty spring flowers. I liked the abbey, but it has nothing to do with Cuthbert. He was never here. Actually he probably did walk through the surrounding fields, but this building didn't exist then – the abbey he joined, and where he happily lived for many years of his life, was a few miles away in a bend in the River Tweed. The name 'Melrose' is said to mean 'bare promontory', and that is where the original abbey was founded. Now there is absolutely nothing to show for it; not even a stone to mark the place. I believe it was destroyed by the Vikings, who delighted in attacking the monasteries since they were full not only of seriously rich treasures, but also holy men and not hardened warriors – a soft touch indeed. So now St Cuthbert's Abbey is only a memory and an empty stretch of ground.

Cuthbert is said to have been about sixteen years old when he joined the monastery because of a vision he had experienced. Not much is known of his early life, and there are several different theories about it. One assumes he was of a noble family because he rode a horse. Another raises the question of why a noble boy would have been watching sheep, which he was, when he had his vision. Also, it is thought he might have been a soldier for a while before joining the monastery. All of these have been woven into his legend. It is also believed he was a Christian from birth, so his parents may have been very early converts from the Anglo-Saxon paganism that was prevalent throughout the kingdom of Northumbria at the time. His dates are circa 634 to the 20th of March 687. We know a foster mother brought him up for some time, and when he went to the monastery to join, he arrived on a horse, hence the 'noble' theories.

But all this was a long time ago and his history will certainly have been embellished a thousandfold over the centuries following his death. There are stories from his childhood that spread through the Christian world, told 'on the authority of Cuthbert' by his brother monks or spoken by those brothers to others. The stories attest to Cuthbert's saintliness. When he was a young boy playing wrestling with his companions, a very little boy of three is said to have run up to him crying that he shouldn't wrestle so, when he was destined to be so holy. Another has Cuthbert a bit older, down by the coast near the mouth of the Tyne River, when he spotted some monks in serious difficulties out at sea. They were moving logs on rafts for their monastery when they were hit by a storm, and were being dragged out to sea. People were standing watching on the shore, jeering at them and not helping, enjoying their desperate plight. Cuthbert was horrified and pleaded with the people to do something to help, or at the very least pray. But the people were happy to see the monks drown, since the Christians had spoken against the old gods of paganism, and they hated this new religion. They would do nothing, so Cuthbert prayed alone, kneeling before the crowd, and at that moment the storm died down, the wind changed and the monks were saved. Bede, the wonderful chronicler of Anglo-Saxon times, said he spoke to a man who had spoken to a man who could swear to it. And in the case of the young, crying child, Bede names his informant – he spoke to *Trumwine of blessed memory told me on the authority of Cuthbert himself*. Bede was a meticulous chronicler, even though he was heavily biased towards the saint.

It is Bede again who tells us the story of Cuthbert's vision. Cuthbert was helping watch a flock of sheep on a hillside, which I subsequently walked over, when he saw something in the night sky. Everyone was asleep but he. Bede says Cuthbert was praying when he saw a streak of light in the darkness coming down to earth, and in the light he discerned angels who, soon after coming down, returned to the heavens with a *spirit of surpassing brightness*. The next day he heard of the death of Aidan, Bishop of Lindisfarne, a man of great holiness, and realised he had been privileged to see the mighty work of God. According to Bede, it was then he resolved to join the monastery. But yet more is recorded of his saintliness, before he even reached Melrose. On his way, riding his horse, he stopped off at a village to ask for food for his horse since it was late in the season for grass. The lady of the house pressed Cuthbert to accept a meal for himself too, since his journey was long and, she said, there were no villages or places for him to find food further on. He refused, stating that since it was a fast day, he could not accept her kind offer at that time. So he rode on and, of course, found himself at last light in the middle of nowhere and hungry. Luckily he spotted an old disused barn so at least he had shelter for his horse and himself, but he was still hungry – the time of fasting now being past. He found some straw for the horse from the roof of the barn – Cuthbert was always noted for his love of animals – and having fed him, knelt down and prayed. While Cuthbert was singing a psalm his horse suddenly pulled a cloth from in amongst the straw and out fell a loaf of bread, still warm, and enough meat for a meal. Thanking God for his bounty, Cuthbert was more than ever convinced of his decision. Bede's informant here was an ancient monk who had this story on Cuthbert's authority too. Bede wrote only as he heard.

The next day was still bright and sunny and our hosts kept telling us how lucky we were, as on previous days, the Eildon Hills, towering over the town on our route out, had been completely shrouded in mist. Now they were standing clear and huge in the morning air – silhouetted majestically in the blue sky high above us. Nothing for it but pull the straps of our backpacks tight, adjust our hats and sunglasses, check our water bottles and be away. We waved a farewell and found the first turning off the road, and onto a well-trodden path leading to the saddle of the Eildon Hills. These huge, almost naked rounded peaks are full of history and folklore. There's archaeological evidence of an enormous hill fort from the Bronze and Iron Ages on the top of the highest peak, which has ramparts of five kilometres and is reckoned to be the capital of the Celtic tribe the Romans called the Selgovae. When the Romans arrived in the 1st century they built a huge fort on the River Tweed just at the foot of the hills, and called it Trimontium in their honour. Rumour has it too that King Arthur of Britain sleeps here with his knights, just waiting for things to get totally apocalyptic before emerging to save us. I saw no Arthur, nor a hoof print in the half-dry mud.

Slowly we ascended to the saddle between the two peaks and gazed about us in delight at the most wonderful scene all around us. Clear and sharp. The new spring green of the growing grasses and leaves and all sorts of plants was fresh and lavish, and just spoke of life and abundance. We looked back at Melrose sitting at the foot of the hills and then forward towards the Cheviots in the far distance and Lindisfarne beyond, a hundred kilometres away. My smile gave away my feelings of pleasure; out in the fresh air with the sun on my face, awake to the natural world about me. The meadow pipits were fluttering about after insects. Over the saddle we walked, and down into the woods of the estate of the Duke of Buccleuch, into the open, shady tracks to emerge into green fields leading to Bowden village, before walking down the banks of the Bowden Burn.

The route of St Cuthbert's Way is, as with all these walks, a modern adaptation based on the stories and legends of where monks and pilgrims walked. The route is chosen for many reasons, but primarily for the simple enjoyment of walking. According to the official guide, it was in very early 1995 that the idea was hatched to create a route to link places attached to the saint. Since it was to cross not only from Scotland into England, but also across numerous people's private land, a huge amount of work went into getting the owners' permissions, let alone the actual waymarking of the route. The waymarking is superb, by the way. I think it was only twice on the entire route that I could have missed the signs, and that was because they were sharp turns onto small paths and easy to simply walk past. I didn't get lost once, and that is a record! The infrastructure – the signs, stiles and gates etc. – are all very well looked after and the route clear and unencumbered; I'm not sure if that's down to route guardians or the private landowners, but it is brilliant. So, having been thought up in 1995, the route was officially opened in 1996 and I was slightly surprised when I read the paragraph in the official guidebook describing it – it says that *at Melrose Abbey, St Cuthbert himself made an appearance after 1,300 years to give the new walk his blessing.* I had to read this a few times and I'm still a bit in the dark about it.

We stopped for tea at Bowden, not because we were thirsty or tired, but because it was too wonderful to hurry, plus there was a nice bench to sit on, but we didn't linger long. On the banks of the burn we walked past Maxpoffle, now a farm but with a glorious name, and not far away is Maxton, which shares its heritage. The name means 'portion of land belonging to Macchus or Magnus'. We know his name, but nothing of him. The next town we came to, following the road from Maxpoffle, was Newtown St Boswells. We know quite a lot of St Boswell, but this Newtown we passed through very quickly, pausing only to let the bus go past on the road we needed to cross. I was amazed as I glanced at the driver; it was the same bus we'd taken the day before, and the driver and I both saw each other at the same time and waved.

The River Tweed is wonderfully beautiful. The sun was still shining strongly, the sky was vivid blue, and the water was sparkling. A few anglers tossed their lines into the stream to see if they could pick up anything. It was a scene of such grandeur and peace.

The route follows the course of the river for a few hundred metres before climbing away into the village of St Boswells itself. I was loath to leave the waterside but the day's destination was far further on and it was already mid morning, so we walked on through St Boswells. We could have, but didn't, cross the river to go and visit Dryburgh Abbey. I was torn. I wanted to do both sides, but in the end the gorgeousness of the river won my heart and I walked away from the abbey.

St Boswell was standing by the gates of Melrose Abbey as Cuthbert arrived after his vision on the hillside. Boswell already had a reputation as a great holy man and Bede suggests that it was he whom Cuthbert wished to be instructed by. However, as Cuthbert walked towards him, still in his layman's clothes, it was Boswell, or Boisil as Bede spells his name, who commented to those near him, "Behold a servant of the Lord", recognising that one day Cuthbert would be a great man of God. Bede heard this from a certain Sigfrid, who was standing near to Boisil on that day. Yet more stories of Cuthbert's burgeoning sainthood. Boisil recommended Cuthbert to the Abbot Eata, and Cuthbert joined them happily and stayed for many years.

Things were not easy for Christians in the 7th century. They were the new kids on the block (forgetting the Christianity brought in by the Romans that had faded to almost nothing with the incoming Anglo-Saxons), and the polytheistic religion of the pagans didn't give up its hold easily. When eventually Christianity became more rooted, a great rift nearly tore it to pieces, and Cuthbert was right in the middle of all this. Traders and travellers and the Roman invasion originally brought Christianity to Britain. When they left and the Northmen invaders arrived, Christianity was pushed into the westernmost extremes. It grew strongly in Wales and south-west England, but it was in Ireland that it was really powerful. The pagan Druidic rituals were replaced by the new religion and the priests were appointed mostly from the powerful royal families of the kingdoms of Ireland.

St Columba was the great-great-grandson of a High King of Ireland. Born on the 7th of December 521, he crossed over to Scotland after his early studies with the Saints Finnian and Ninian, and founded a monastery on the island of Iona. This area of Scotland was part of the great Irish kingdom of Dál Riata. The monastery was famed throughout the land for its teaching, and was probably the most important religious centre in Western Europe at the time. Iona flourished and became rich. It crowned kings and buried them too, and in 616 it became the home in exile of a young Prince of Northumbria, brought by his mother for safety. Oswald was the son of the King Æthelfrith, the King of Bernicia and Deira, and his Queen Acha. Æthelfrith was killed in a battle by King Rædwald of East Anglia. Acha then fled with her children to sanctuary before the new king, her brother Edwin, could kill them. There Oswald grew to manhood and became a Christian.

Northumbria, comprising Bernicia and Deira, the two great kingdoms of the Anglo-Saxon age, was staunchly pagan. The Anglo-Saxons brought their gods with them: Thor, Odin, Balder, Freya and more. The northern kingdom had so far resisted the spread of Christianity from the south. The Gregorian mission had arrived in Kent in 597, bringing in Christianity when the King of Kent, Æthelberht, married the Christian daughter of the King of the Franks. Christianity flourished in Kent and a second wave of missionaries arrived in 601. Amongst this second wave was the monk Paulinus. Bede described him as *a tall man with a slight stoop, who had black hair, a thin face, a narrow aquiline nose, his presence being venerable and awe-inspiring.* He joined Augustine and remained in Canterbury until 625.

It was then that Edwin, the King of Northumbria and successor to Æthelfrith, sent a message to Eadbald, the King of Kent, with a wish to marry his sister, Æthelburg. Eadbald refused, pointing out that he could not allow a Christian princess to marry a pagan. Edwin responded by telling Eadbald that Æthelburg would be free to worship as her conscience led her to, and hinted that he might even think about converting himself. The marriage went ahead and Paulinus accompanied the new queen as her chaplain. He was also aware he was in a brilliant position to convert the heathen northerners, and the king too. It worked, and Edwin was baptised in York in 627, along with reputedly

3000 others it took thirty-six days to do them all. Edwin's dual kingdom of Northumbria collapsed following his death and he was succeeded in Deira by Osric, a cousin of his, and by Eanfrith in Bernicia. Eanfrith was the eldest son of Æthelfrith and brother of Oswald, and had also been brought up on Iona. On taking over their two kingdoms, which were in chaos, they both reverted to paganism.

All this time Oswald had been biding his time on Iona, watching and waiting. Eventually in 633 or 634 he came out of exile, and met Eanfrith and Osric's killer, Cadwallon, King of Gwynedd, at the battle of Heavenfield near Hexham. Before the battle Oswald is said to have had a huge wooden cross erected, which he and his army prayed before. He won the battle and took over all of the dual kingdom of Northumbria. One of his first acts as king was to send messengers back to Iona, to ask for a mission to come into his kingdom. Oswald was a Christian and he wanted his people to join him in the new religion. Iona was more than happy to do so. They sent a band of brothers led by the monk Corman. Things did not go well. Corman returned to Iona within months, complaining that the Northumbrians were barbarians, stupid even, and would not learn anything! The community of Iona were not impressed. This was a serious situation. It was a quiet monk sitting listening to Corman ranting who asked the question: "Brother, couldn't you have been a bit gentler?" That question sealed the monk's destiny. Aidan was his name, and the community decided he would go and try again, in a gentler way than Brother Corman. So, in the year that Cuthbert was born, Aidan set out to convert the pagans of the northern kingdom.

The kingdom of Northumbria is no more (St Boswells is in the Scottish Borders), and Aidan was successful in his mission although it wasn't easy. For ourselves we needed ice creams, and walking through St Boswells we found a delightful shop that sold whatever we wanted. Licking our deliciousness, we walked back down to the Tweed and along through the immaculate golf course that follows the southern bank on our way. We followed the riverbank down past a weir and an old mill, now converted for fishermen, and by a salmon ladder. No fish were leaping, as the water was low. We walked over a bridge and stopped for a while to rest our feet in the cool water and watch the oystercatchers on the other bank, and a young cygnet and its parents poking about in the reeds. On the Duke of Sutherland's land across the river were rows of poplars that were a wonderful sight. We walked in sunshine and saw no one; alone, just us. I pondered that Cuthbert would have loved this place, and would have stopped to pray. I had heard another story of Cuthbert. He and a fellow monk, a young, inexperienced novice, were going out to seek converts. After walking for some time they were hungry, and the novice was complaining they had no food. Cuthbert, remembering God's bounty in the barn on his way to Melrose, told the novice to have faith. Just then an eagle dropped a salmon not far from them as they sat by the river. "Hurrah!" shouted the novice, and rushed to collect the fish. Cuthbert told him to stop, cut the fish in half and give half to the eagle to say thank you.

It was at a place called Crystal Waters, where a spring comes out of the ground, that we finally climbed away from the lovely river, up a flight of steps and into a cool, shady wood of mixed trees which dropped down again into more woods overfilled with wild garlic. We were quiet at this stage, chattering stopped for a while as we walked in single file through the white-flowered green bed of garlic, when we saw, standing very still, a full-grown female roe deer. As we stood and looked at her, and she at us, she slowly turned and gracefully jumped over the carpet of green and was away, further into the trees and out of our sight. It was a wonderful moment. I knew that somewhere in this wood was a sacred spring (an unannounced, overgrown spring), but we didn't find it. Instead we emerged into bright sunlight, again by the kirk at Maxton. It's been here as a place of worship for over a thousand years, and was referred to as St Cuthbert's Church of Mackistun.

The path continued now on road – firstly just a gravelled path used by the congregation, and then onto a small road, which took us away from the trees and towards the thundering A68. It is inevitable that all walks will include a noisy highway. The Romans came to Britain. They built roads. They built fantastic roads that went in arrow-straight lines between their towns and forts, and they built them very well indeed. The legacy they left is a collection of arteries through the landscape that were still used centuries after the Romans departed. And now, a couple of thousand years later, these roads have in many cases become our network of motorways all over Britain. The A68 is one such as it follows the route of Dere Street. Dere Street went from York to the old Antonine Wall in Scotland, to Edinburgh and the Firth of Forth. On St Cuthbert's Way we walked along it for about six kilometres (luckily not a part that has been included in the A68). Dere Street has its own waymarkers – a cute centurion's helmet which replaced the Cross of St Cuthbert for this stretch. We needed them as there were mostly just a few rocks and stones to show us where the path actually was – I presume the stones have been taken over the years to build walls and shelters. Anyway, we walked parallel to the A68, having to listen to the noise of vehicles tearing along it.

To start with we walked through woods, but then we skirted fields, over stiles and through gates. The path wound on up and down gentle hills and through brightly flowering gorse. I've never seen gorse so bright, nor had I ever smelt any sort of perfume from it. The gentle breeze wafted over to us the strange and completely unexpected scent of coconut. It reminded us of the early forms of suntan lotion that fried our skin in the sun. At first we were confused, but it really was the gorse.

Some way down the track is a monument, a coffin-shaped stone, to commemorate a local woman, Lady Lilliard, who fought at the Battle of Ancrum in 1545 after the English had killed her lover. The inscription says it all:

Fair maiden Lilliard lays under this stane,
Little was her stature but muckle was her fame,
Upon the English loons she laid many thumps,
And when her legs were cuttit off, she fought upon her stumps…

We stopped to admire the incredible view – behind us we saw the Eildon Hills many miles away, and ahead the first glimpse of the Cheviots.

Dere Street seemed rather long, but eventually we arrived, at the end of our first day, at the Harestanes Visitor Centre. Since there's nowhere to stay here – nothing at all except for the visitor centre – we turned left and walked into the village of Ancrum. As a village it isn't that big, but it does have a pub and one general store, and it was here we were staying, at the Ancrum Barn. It turned out to be the most wonderful night's rest I could imagine. I think the barn must have been the cowshed originally, but now the owners of the local shop, the Ancrum Pantry, have fitted it out with two and a half beds, a great little bathroom and a sitting room with everything you could think to want. And not only that, but they open at 6.30am and will cook a bacon sandwich and provide wonderful coffee – heavenly.

Yesterday, on the walk on Dere Street, we'd met a couple of men who told us that the abbey in Jedburgh was marvellous and that we'd be crazy to miss it. OK, we said, we wouldn't, so we caught the bus and found we were massively early for anything – only the postman was about. Thankfully one bakery was open that had a couple of tables inside, so we drank more coffee and ate more food and waited for the abbey to wake up. It is a glorious shell of a ruin that was enhanced by the day's dazzling blue sky. So, having looked around and poked into the crevices, so to speak, and looked at the very good museum, we got a ride to continue our walk.

We were dropped off at Morebattle. We'd lost a few miles of the Way, but we were determined to walk the stretch that had been described to us by several people we'd spoken to as the jewel of the whole route. From Morebattle we walked over a small rise and onto the flattish valley, just in front of a massive ridge that rose steeply in front of us. I whistled – it is *steep*. It's not even very gradual, in fact it goes from flat walking to uphill crawling in a few short metres, but again every breath was worth it. In fact, it is worth stopping every short while to take in the view back as well as to have a breather, because it's so lovely. I was aware of course that in a black storm it may not have been so incredible, but we were again blessed by warm sunshine and a slight breeze, just enough to cool us as we trudged uphill.

Away to our right was marshy ground that had been known as Linton Loch. Linton Loch was the home of the Linton Worm. This worm, or *Wyrm*, was a great serpent-dragon that killed and ate anything and everything. That was, until it was fooled and killed by the brave Sir John Somerville in the 12th century. His family has now a dragon on its crest. As it was dying the dragon slipped back into its lair, and thrashing about in its death throes, brought down the mountain, burying it inside. The curious geography hereabouts has sometimes been called Wormington in memory of the Linton Worm. More factually, Wideopen Hill is the northernmost ridge of the Cheviot Hills that are associated with a collision of the continents Laurentia and Avalonia. This was approximately 400 million years ago, and it resulted in quite an upheaval with volcanic activity. Factual, but not half as poetic as the Linton Worm by a long way.

From a standing start up to a fantastic view, walking to the top of the world to gaze at the big, wide-open spaces of Wideopen Hill. At 368 metres it is the highest point on St Cuthbert's Way, and it is about halfway along too. Rarely have I enjoyed anything so much as arriving at the summit of Wideopen Hill. We stopped and stared and didn't say a word to each other except to say, "Let's not go down yet; let's sit awhile." So we did. We ate an orange each and just sighed with pleasure.

Standing again, we strode down the other side, through fields of new lambs and fresh grass, into the valley below towards Bowmont Water and the small hamlet of Town Yetholm, where we hadn't really meant to stop. The pub was open and the benches empty, so we sat and enjoyed a pie and a half a pint and chatted to the girl who ran the place. Sitting in the afternoon sun was very relaxing and our night's beds were close by, one mile away in Kirk Yetholm.

We found our host working on a new house next to his B&B, single-handedly, it seemed to us, creating a whole new suburb to this tiny village. Charles was generous to a fault and we had the place to ourselves. The pub (another one, where he directed us to for our supper) was the Border Hotel that acts as the official end of the Pennine Way. I think it is more popular as a fishing destination than for walkers. They had masses of delicious-looking fish dishes on their fabulous menu – no fasting here – and the wallpaper in their dining room bore a pattern of a plethora of fish. I got chatting to a chap in the bar who told me something of the story of Kirk Yetholm; that it was the home of Scotland's gypsies. The story goes that a gypsy man saved the life of a Captain David Bennet, who was a local landowner in 1695. In gratitude Bennet gave some land to the gypsies, and they came to stay, in safety. (A law in 1609 had made it legal to kill gypsies in Scotland.) They remained fiercely proud of their ethnic identity until 1898 when the last 'king' of the gypsies died, and the rest became simply Scottish. There is a memorial to them on the village green.

Onward on St Cuthbert's Way, and on towards England. Kirk Yetholm is only one mile from the English border, and reaching it meant more delightful tramps on grassy paths up hillsides and along contours. We were also following the route of the Pennine Way here, with its acorn waymarkers. The ground was often very boggy, and we had to step around some particularly bad areas, or jump from tussock to tussock. We continued the Pennine Way until a waymarker took us off and towards the north-east rather than due east. We passed by Green Humbleton Hill, with its ancient Iron Age hill fort on the summit that was surrounded by skylarks, and while we were still high in the Cheviot Hills, we crossed over from the Scottish Borders and into the Northumberland National Park and England.

As I walked along, enjoying the sunshine and watching the newborn lambs, I tried to imagine Cuthbert coming out into these hills to spread the word of God but honestly I could feel nothing – there was too much else to think about, so I gave up looking for dead monks and concentrated on the view. The gorse was growing thickly as we dropped down to Hethpool. Lambs were being born all around us and the farmers were dashing about on their quad bikes, trying to help where they could. We spotted one sheep across the field that was standing with head bowed, simply looking at the white blob of her lamb that was lying as still as could be. We wished it would move, but in the time it took us to walk by, it did not. The farmer whizzed past and asked us to come back next year if we would again bring such fine weather with us.

Hethpool turned out to be one farm, a large farm with a couple of Arts and Crafts cottages too, but nothing else. From there we dropped into the College Valley – the name is thought to be from the Anglo-Saxon *col* and *leche* which together mean 'a stream flowing through marshy ground'. It's held in trust, which restricts all vehicles to twelve per day and none at all in lambing season, so it's lovely and quiet. The word 'bucolic' actually came to my mind as I stood on the bridge, taking in the vista around me.

Climbing out of the College Valley on the other side, we walked along in front of the three tors of Hare Law, Wester Tor and Easter Tor, before winding our way up the steep side of Easter Tor into the northern Cheviot Hills. Apparently this place has feral goats that have been roaming about on the slopes of Easter Tor and the neighbouring

Yeavering Bell for centuries. The massive hill fort that sits astride Yeavering Bell is believed to have been the stronghold of the Votadini tribe, whom the Romans would have known and probably fought too. The hill fort is older than Roman times and very large, five hectares surrounded by a wall around one kilometre long. Archaeology has unearthed up to 130 hut circles within the fort. It must have been a major settlement in its time.

More recently in 627, Paulinus was here. This is the site of King Edwin's great palace of Ad Gefrin, and it is here that Paulinus is said to have baptised three thousand Northumbrians in the nearby River Glen.

The route stayed on the high ground and we walked on into the open countryside and in the sunshine. For the last couple of days I had been wearing a short-sleeved shirt, and now I was suffering the effects of the sun: my right arm was sunburnt! Only my right arm, as of course we were walking almost exclusively west to east, so with the sun further south my right side was exposed. It was burning; it hurt. I tried to cover it but nothing really worked, and I was glad when the clouds bubbled up and blocked the sun, if only for a few brief moments. The views were breathtaking still, and walking on, we had to stop every now and again to appreciate where we were.

The guidebook warned us that in bad weather this stretch of the walk was very dangerous. It would be easy to get lost in heavy snow or thick mist, and in such circumstances it would be better to walk on the road, but we had no such trouble. We tramped past Tom Tallon's Crag and jumped from tussock to tussock to boardwalk through an area called the Trows that was formed beneath the ice when the Cheviot Icefield melted some ten thousand years ago. Not all of the water has gone yet. To our left, the guidebook told me, was Humbleton Hill that was the site of the Battle of Homilton in 1402 – Shakespeare referred to it in his play *Henry IV, Part 1*.

Eventually, after several kilometres of walking next to patches of woodland and high across open hills, we dropped down into a wood and then into the town of Wooler itself. What a metropolis it seemed! Wooler is the biggest settlement on St Cuthbert's Way; it's a real town and has several pubs, restaurants and shops, and lots of people. It sits in a tight valley and is still an important market town for the district. Its weekly livestock market is, apparently, the most important in the north-east of Britain. Originally named Well on the Hill, the place has been here since the Stone Age, and the Romans liked the site too. They reused the Iron Age settlement of Kettles just above the town. We found our beds for the night in the Black Bull pub and, after a nice supper and a gentle evening reading and writing diaries, went to bed with tired legs and a great sense of achievement and enjoyment from a wonderful day.

On to the next day, and I needed sunscreen – my arm was on fire. So it was a slightly delayed morning start, waiting for the chemist to come to life. Eventually we were away, past the 12th-century Church of St Mary and up the other side of the valley, climbing onto Weetwood Bank and thus onto Weetwood Moor. This moor marks the end of the Cheviot Hills. We were no longer walking on the result of ancient continents colliding. Now we were on the Fell Sandstone moorland, which lies between the Cheviots and the coastal plain. This sandstone is a pretty pink and is popular as a building material.

We had read about the prehistoric cup-and-ring petroglyphs carved into the flat rock boulders strewn about up here, and we were keen to try and find them. The directions we had were so unspecific that we failed. We walked around for ages but stone after stone was unmarked, so we gave up and walked on. It was all quite different – the landscape. It was softer, more rounded and gentler than the Cheviots. The route on the moor wasn't far and, passing a couple of plantations, the path took us over the lip of a valley, and down through new stands of deciduous trees and a superb view into the Till Valley and Weetwood Bridge. This bridge, recently restored, was the route of the Earl of Surrey and his men on their way to the bloody Battle of Flodden in 1513. No armies now came to clatter over, but one car did make us stand back before allowing us to cross over to Weetwood Hall and ahead to Doddington Moor. The cool of the morning was wearing off and the sun was peeking out between the clouds, and walking on the road meant that I could go into a daydream, not worrying about my next footfall. I wanted to be aware of where I was, as here was the meadow where Cuthbert had had his vision. I looked at the sheep in the fields and imagined it: a young man watching the flock, keeping them from harm. All his fellow watchers were asleep, and he alone saw the bright light descend and collect the spirit of St Aidan. I can't imagine what he thought, but surely he must have been frightened. I guess the bright light was a fireball of some sort, lightning or even a falling meteorite. Whatever the bright light was, it brought Cuthbert to a decision that has had an effect on many others for centuries.

I was beginning to get a little excited now. The map told me that we were getting nearer to St Cuthbert's Cave. There's not much to connect Cuthbert to the route besides the meadow and the cave. I felt that, walking to Wooler over the high, tussocked hills, he would have delighted in the wildness of the scene; that the weather could turn in a moment to raging storms. Here, on the other hand, it was sunny and sweet. The flowers were waving in the gentle breeze, the daffodils still in bloom. The gorse was still bright yellow, as was the rape in the vast fields. For a few miles we could see, high over on the next hillside, several stands of trees that, according to my map, marked where the cave should be. The waymarkers kept leading us down trodden paths through fields, one after another, and we kept guessing which stand of trees we would be led on to. On we went until finally we were in amongst a stand of pines, and then we saw the cave on a slight rise up on our right. There it was, up a gentle hill and through an avenue of trees. It was bigger than I had expected, and the boulders next to the main cave fascinated me. They had deep clefts incised into the sloping sides, caused, I presumed, by thousands of years of water erosion. Fancifully, though, I thought, *What if, instead of ordinary rainwater erosion, thousands upon thousands of pilgrims over the centuries came and cried for their saint, and caused, by those tears, these deep marks down the rock?* In the stories of Cuthbert's post-mortem travels in 875 it is not clear how long the monks stayed at the cave, with Cuthbert in his coffin. I wondered if the coffin was of lead. Lead is very heavy, and even if the monks were very strong it would be quite a task to carry it. In any case, it was a deed of great devotion.

The body's journey took many years, and the monks under Bishop Eardulf of Lindisfarne were running from the Viking raids, afraid that Cuthbert, as well as their greatest treasure, the Gospels of Lindisfarne, would fall into heathen hands. After this resting place, they travelled to Cumberland, southern Scotland, Ripon and on, but when the coffin was on a ship to Ireland it rained blood. This portent suggested to the poor exhausted monks that the saint didn't want to go to Ireland. So back they went to England and Scotland and back to England until eventually ending up in Durham. Back at the cave, we nosed about reading the graffiti, some of which is very old, and then sat and had our lunch leaning up against the cold stone and looking at the view.

We were in no hurry other than wishing to see the sea, so after a while of closing our eyes in the sunshine, we got up and moved off and at the top of the next hill, we saw, hazily in the distance, the Holy Island shimmering on the horizon; a pale brown smear surrounded by blue. A few miles still to go, and here we found a new waymarker to follow, as well as the Cross of St Cuthbert. We were joined by St Oswald's Way that runs from Lindisfarne to his battlefield at Heavenfield, some 156 kilometres away. Together the two paths took us through some more woodland. This was Shiellow Wood, part of the woodland known as Kyloe Old Wood. The Leyland family of Haggerston Estate, who developed some of the original leylandii cypress stock, owned the woods in the 19th century. Luckily for the woodland manager's team today, the wood doesn't have any leylandii that we could see, but it is an open, well-tended pine forest. We walked down the broad paths, listening to the wind in the branches above us. All this area provided the priory at Lindisfarne with the provisions they needed to survive. The monks dug peat for fuel from the far side of Shiellow Wood, and the ancient rhyme tells us:

From Goswick we've geese, from Cheswick we've cheese,
From Buckton we've venison in store,
From Swinhoe we've bacon, but the Scots have taken,
And the Prior is longing for more.

Down the road is the village of Beal, the name being a shortening of 'Bee Hill', from where the monks had their honey which, very importantly, was the essential ingredient for their mead.

A lot of people, when they reach here to get to the Holy Island, are in panic over the tides, but we had decided to spend the night on the mainland, so we had an easy stroll down to the village of Fenwick, and its only B&B. What a super B&B it was too. Not only was our hostess really, really lovely, but she very kindly turned on the heating when I turned up downstairs wearing my down jacket! She had two couples staying besides us, so there were six of us who all asked her for supper since there was nowhere to eat nearby, and we had a cheery evening chatting over a fantastic meal, and again at breakfast too.

Breakfast was a bit of a moan. We'd had bright, sunny, clear days ever since Melrose and now, when we would have totally appreciated sunshine, we had instead heavy, soaking rain and strong winds. It started before dawn and carried on and on, and even if I was eternally optimistic that it was clearing, it never let up. We sat for ages hoping, but eventually we just had to move on, and as the saying goes, there's no such thing as bad weather, just bad clothing. In wet 'proofs, and with good wishes ringing in our ears from our fellow guests, we sloshed off down the road.

The first obstacle was the busy Great North Road, and with a quick dash we made it over, to be faced by the East Coast Main Line rail track. I had instructions for how to get over. I picked up the handset in the yellow phone box and after a few rings a man's voice barked at me, asking for my location.

"Er…" After a few false starts, I spotted the word Fenham on the sign by the phone.

"OK," said the voice, "you wait – the Virgin train is coming."

Very true. The roar was growing as we spoke, and in a few minutes it thundered past, towering above us, so much bigger than they seem when they're sitting by the platform in a station.

"Now," said the voice, "cross over and call me from the other side."

So we ran and I phoned and we were free – no more obstacles. The rain was still driving into my face and dribbling down my neck, and climbing through a gate, we were on the road to the crossing over to the Holy Island. It was hard to look squarely at it with the rain, but one thing was clear: the tide was still too high to cross. There was no cover here at all, only a car park and an information board and signs telling people to simply not chance it with the tides and to wait until it was safe to cross. We couldn't just stand there in the rain and get even wetter and colder, so we sought sanctuary from the elements. Strung out across the sand are the refuges put up to save pilgrims caught in the rising tidal waters. The first one is conveniently on the road causeway. We scrambled up, me hanging on to the handrails and hoping the whipping wind wouldn't take me off into the water – receding, yes, but still looking very cold.

In a shelter and out of the rain, it looked as if it would be ages until the sands were dry enough for us to cross – I had planned to walk that way, but in the end I simply didn't have the patience to wait one and a half hours in this cold and uncomfortable box, so after a quick discussion we headed off down the road causeway. The wind blew hard and the sound of the rain hitting the water filled my ears as I kept my head down, keeping close to the road's edge as a few cars drove by. The water lapped at the road, but the closer we got to the hard land of the island it receded, and the weather cleared, too – the rain let up and the wind died down.

We made it. We arrived. Very few people were there –it was only midday – but more would come in the afternoon as the tide went all the way out. The one road onto the island fed into a car park where all visitors are asked to leave their vehicles. We walked on to what I think was the main street, called Marygate. It had cottages, a post office and a heritage centre that told the story of the island. Many of the cottages were B&Bs, but we were staying in the pub. I asked the way of a woman out with her dog, who said, "Past the church and past the winery", and sure enough, there it was. The Crown and Anchor was right next to the priory. What a position. As I lay on my bed later I could see the ruined walls some forty metres away, no more than that. Splendid.

Cuthbert was very happy in Melrose, doing the odd miracle, meeting angels and similar. Melrose was a sister house to Aidan's great monastery at Lindisfarne, so Cuthbert was trained in the Irish tradition, the Celtic Christian rituals. Celtic Christianity, as opposed to Roman Christianity, which was beginning to gain some powerful adherents. Melrose was offered land in Ripon by the king to build another sister house, and Cuthbert was sent there to be the guest-master under Bishop Eata. It was during this time when a man turned up at the monastery to be met by Cuthbert, who welcomed him graciously, washing his feet (a greeting all strangers received) before going off to get some fresh bread for the stranger. When he returned, however, the place was empty, and looking out into the freshly fallen snow there were no footprints to be seen, but sitting on the table were three fresh loaves of bread –

Cuthbert apparently often chatted to angels, according to Bede. But all was not well at Ripon. A new bishop took over from Eata, a certain Bishop Wilfrid or Wilfrith. He wanted things done a little bit differently to how they were run at Melrose and indeed at Lindisfarne.

Wilfrid was a Northumbrian noble, and as a young man had studied at Lindisfarne. Unlike many of his contemporaries he went further in both his studies and his travels. He is often described as being very ambitious, and became very attracted to the Roman way of doing things. He spent time in Canterbury before going on pilgrimage to Rome, with the already well-travelled Bishop Biscop. Wilfrid parted company with Biscop in Gaul, where he stayed for some time, narrowly avoiding being married off to the archbishop's daughter and being made into a provincial governor. He refused such a life and carried on to Rome. His hagiographer, Stephen of Ripon, tells us that in Rome Wilfrid learned of the Roman way, which meant, amongst other things, the method of calculating Easter, which differed so markedly from the Celtic tradition back home. He was apparently overawed by the scale of the churches and monasteries of Rome, their richness and brilliance when compared with the rough and basic monasteries back home. He was in no hurry to return but, having had his audience with the pope, he did go back to Gaul. He continued to follow the Roman way there for about three years.

On his return to Britain in 658, Cenwalh, the King of Wessex, recommended Wilfrid to Alhfrith, who was sub-ruler of Deira. Alhfrith 'gifted' the monastery at Ripon to Wilfrid in 661, thereby ousting the Abbot Eata. Immediately there was friction. Eata had come from Melrose, and had taken Cuthbert with him. He had been trained in the Celtic tradition, having studied with the great St Aidan himself, and he had no wish to follow the Roman way, so Wilfrid promptly expelled him. Cuthbert and Eata then returned to Melrose. Bede simply recorded the facts with no mention of feelings, although he did say Eata was a very gentle and holy man, and greatly respected. So Cuthbert went back to

Melrose where St Boisil was in charge. Three years later, the 'yellow plague' ravished the country and the monastery too, and Boisil died. It was exactly as he had prophesied, and again as he prophesied, Cuthbert was appointed prior in his stead.

The tension between the traditional practices and the new was developing into discord in Britain in the 7th century. The Celtic ways of Columba and Aidan were at loggerheads with the Roman approach, now followed by Wilfrid and Biscop and many others. It caused much dissent and rifts within the Church while it was trying to convert the heathens away from paganism. There were many differences, but one of the most difficult was Easter. The Celtic Church had calculated the date to celebrate the resurrection of Christ in line with the Jewish traditions of the very earliest churches. This was rather complicated – it had to be concurrent with the Jewish festival of Passover, which was on the fourteenth day of the first lunar month of the Jewish year on the day of the crucifixion according to John 19:14. This meant it often fell on a day that wasn't Sunday – the day of the Resurrection. The Council of Nicea in 325, called by Constantine, decreed the Church should abandon the Jewish calendar. An even more complicated system was then devised, so the celebration always fell on a Sunday. Other differences were the monastic tonsure and manner of penance, and the practice of living an eremitic life away from the monastery and the rule of the Church.

It all came to a head soon after Wilfrid took over at Ripon. King Oswiu of Northumbria, who followed the Celtic custom, was married to Queen Eanflæd. She, as a mentor and advocate of Wilfrid, practised the Roman way. This meant that when the king and his court were finished with Lent and were feasting and celebrating the Resurrection, the queen and her court were still in deep mourning, fasting and praying in Lent. Previously this hadn't been an issue, but Alhfrith, son and heir apparent to Oswiu, caused his father to call a solution for this 'problem'. So in 664 King Oswiu convened a synod at the great monastery under the Abbess Hilda at Whitby.

Stephen of Ripon tells us about it in his hagiography, as does the redoubtable Bede a short while later in the *Anglo-Saxon Chronicle*. The Synod of Whitby of 664 was a turning point in the history of the Church in Britain, but it had more to it than just religious practices. Britain was beginning to look outwards again after the Dark Ages following the Romans' withdrawal. For a couple of centuries internal problems had meant that the Continent was to a large extent ignored. But the more settled peace of the 7th century allowed freer trade and more movement of people everywhere. The Church was always influential in more ways than simply church matters, and it has been suggested that King Oswiu may well have been looking at greater trade opportunities, and alliances with fellow kings abroad. Hence worshipping in the same rituals and practices would have been advantageous, especially when making marriage propositions to seal alliances.

On the Celtic side of the polemic was the Bishop of Northumbria, Colmán, and on the Roman side was the Frankish Bishop Agilbert. Agilbert's English wasn't up to the complicated debate needed, so Wilfrid was chosen to speak on his behalf. Many issues were discussed but the deciding factor was simple – King Oswiu was told that St Peter held the keys to Heaven, given to him by Christ himself. Oswiu concluded, then, that since it was Peter who held the keys, he could theoretically refuse him entry to Heaven. This struck him as being a possible problem. Plus, said Oswiu, since St Peter was the 'rock' of the Church and its first bishop in Rome, Roman Christianity was therefore the true religion and he decided for Wilfrid's side.

The followers of the Celtic tradition were devastated and many couldn't accept the ruling, including Colmán who, with many others, left for Iona to worship as they had always done. Cuthbert was different. Although he loved the Church of his teachers, he loved the unity of the Church more. His old friend Eata, again the abbot of Melrose and who was also in charge of Lindisfarne, asked him to become the prior there and try to reconcile the monks and bring peace after such a cataclysmic upset. It was a hard time for the Church. Cuthbert was well chosen for the job, with his intellect and humble manner, but still it took a long time and much patience to persuade his brother monks away from the old way of doing things, and to accept the new rule of monasticism. That the priory here survived and subsequently grew even more in importance is all testament to his abilities as prior.

It was here, I thought as I lay on my bed looking at the ruins of his priory, that Cuthbert really became the 'fire of the North'. Bede tells us he travelled widely all over the countryside, praying and leading his people. Bede also says he cured the sick of body with his touch and the sick of mind with his sympathetic ear. People started to flock to Lindisfarne to see him. The small island must have been very crowded, and consequently grew in riches.

By the time we arrived and sorted ourselves out, not only had the cars started arriving over the now completely dry causeway, but the sun had come back out. We walked out to see where we were. The village consists of about 160 residents, three coffee houses, three pubs, one post office and the heritage centre, as well as the priory museum and bookshop and a few shops selling such things as St Aidan's mead and locally made fudge (yum). We made immediately for the priory. I had to look around the bookshop first, but the museum attached, which is more of an information centre dedicated to the saint himself, was outstanding. It gives the story of the Anglo-Saxons, the Viking raids and the journey of St Cuthbert's body until his final resting place at Durham. It was the Viking raids that sent Cuthbert on his posthumous meanderings.

We carried on and into the priory itself, and I wandered about, sad that this wasn't the original priory – the same story as at Melrose: destroyed by the raiding Vikings. Lindisfarne under Cuthbert became the most famous priory in the north, and stories of the man himself grew, but he was a reclusive man who needed time to himself. On one occasion he decided to visit his friend, the Abbess Ebbe at Coldingham, to be alone and to pray. One night he was spotted by a monk as he was sneaking out of the monastery and going down to the beach. The monk, intrigued, followed and watched Cuthbert pray all night, up to his neck in the cold waters of the North Sea. When he emerged at dawn two otters came up to him and dried him with their breath until at his signal they disappeared back into the sea. Bede again tells us the monk admitted he'd been spying but Cuthbert didn't scold him, just asked him not to tell anyone while he was still alive. However, on Cuthbert's death he told everyone who would listen.

The ruins now are all that remain, and are a rich red sandstone that has weathered into the most beautiful mosaic-type patterns – almost as though on purpose. The bright green grass is closely cropped around the stones, showing the outlines of the room foundations themselves, and information boards give a small amount of detail as to what was where. The original wooden building was erected around 635, but when the Vikings arrived in 793, the priory suffered badly. The final straw was in 875 when, after years of successive raids, the terrified monks could endure no more and left, taking the remains of St Cuthbert with them. The priory fell to ruin and it wasn't until 1083 that the site was refounded and the present stone building put up. The community stayed here until King Henry VIII's Dissolution. Henry himself later plundered much of the priory's stone to build the castle nearby. He needed a defensive position to keep the invading Scots at bay and by 1549 he had a fort built on the highest part of the island, called Beblowe Craig. He had used the priory as a weapons depot after dissolving the church as well as pilfering the stone for the walls.

In one corner of the priory stands a modern statue of St Cuthbert – the only one I had seen anywhere as I had followed his pilgrimage route from Melrose to the Holy Island. Next to the priory stands the

Church of St Mary the Virgin – the present-day parish church which is said to be on the exact spot of Aidan's original wooden church. The site itself nestles well within a sort of hollow with a ridge known as the Heugh, protecting the buildings, and in fact the whole town, from the sea. I walked up on the Heugh and gazed around at the surrounding water. There's an observation tower too, which gives a wonderful high perspective over everything. Over to the right of the priory is the natural harbour of the Ouse, which appeared to be mostly unused. A few fishing boats were drawn up on the shingle beach and an array of lobster pots stacked about. The huts on the beach were upturned boats with doors cut into them. But the great basalt outcrop dominates the view, with the castle perched high above the surrounding land. To the other side of the tower I had my first glimpse of the little island that St Cuthbert retired to initially; it is called Hobthrush, and also St Cuthbert's Islet. The tide was out and it barely looked like an island.

I enjoyed that we were staying on the island, as eventually all the day trippers had to leave as the tide inched its way up and over the causeway and the sand again. We had a lovely evening in our pub, in particular loving the fact it had a bath rather than a shower. To soak one's feet after a few days of walking is such a delight.

Early the next day, after an delicious breakfast we were out and about, and we seemed to be the only ones. I suppose since no one can cross over until low tide, and at this time of year that fell just before midday, the locals seemed to think there wasn't much point in rising early. It was great, though. We walked along the wet sand and out into the dunes to the north of the island. Here the landscape is really very different. Whereas around the town is flat farming and sheep, to the north in the prevailing weather on the windward side of the island, the sand is piled up into high, tussock-covered dunes. We found paths through the marram grass and walked over them to the huge, wide-open space of the beach. So beautiful, and so empty.

The coast is more rugged and rocky on the north-east side, which means that the raiders would have automatically sailed around to the quieter lee of the island and into the natural harbour of the Ouse – very easy to raid the nearby priory. We walked on around the island, enjoying the sunshine and the walk and listening to the birds calling as we trod close to their nests – careful not to disturb any.

Lindisfarne is also a major stopping-off place for many migrating birds, and thus is a birdwatchers' paradise. Over three hundred species have been recorded on the mudflats and the salt marshes. A large part of the island has been turned into a nature reserve and every autumn, 40% of the world's population of light-bellied brent geese come and visit, escaping their usual grounds in cold northern Svalbard. We stopped for a while to watch a swan in the reeds but it was asleep so there wasn't much to see, and the black-headed gulls weren't doing much either. It was very peaceful though as we stood by a lake in the low-lying area to the west of the island. Cuthbert loved these birds as he loved all animals. There are several stories of his connection with other creatures, and especially with birds. One local species of eider duck is named after him – Cuddy's duck (the name 'Cuddy' is the Northumbrian familiar of Cuthbert's name).

In no time at all we had walked the entire way around the island and found ourselves outside the castle. The original building was Henry's fort soon after he dissolved the priory on this amazing stack of basalt. The fort fell into disrepair after the Scots were subdued and it wasn't needed any longer. It was only brought back to life in 1902 when Edward Hudson, the magazine magnate who started up *Country Life* magazine, bought the place. He commissioned the fashionable architect Edwin Lutyens to convert it as a holiday home for himself and his guests. The National Trust now owns it and has opened it to the public. We climbed the hill and bought our tickets and spent a cheerful hour or so poking about.

Bede writes in his *Life of St Cuthbert* that the saint won over the disgruntled monks with his patience and modesty. But his work to convert the people as he travelled over the countryside has given us many stories of his miracles. Two of them involve fire. Once when he was preaching the word of God in a village, Cuthbert saw the spirit of the Devil amongst the crowd. He exhorted them to listen to him and not heed the temptations of evil. As he said this a fire sprang up at a neighbouring house. People rushed to put it out, but their water had no effect on the flames. The fire only died away when Cuthbert prayed and evil *was put to flight*. Another tale mentions his foster mother, whom he was visiting. Her house was at the western end of the village, and when he entered and started talking of the word of God, the eastern end of the village caught alight. The villagers tried to put it out, but the heat was too intense. A woman ran to Cuthbert to ask his help. He assured her that all would be well, and at that he prostrated himself on the ground and, as with the monks in peril out at sea, the wind changed direction again and flames died out. Bede says Cuthbert cured many by the touch of his hand alone – people both noble and rich, and poor and ragged.

But Cuthbert's severe regime of fasting and praying, never stopping in his efforts to spread the word of God, as well as instil love for the new rites of the Church, took its toll and he yearned for solitude and contemplation. He was granted permission to retire. There are several suggestions as to where he went to live his hermitic life. Some say he lived on the tiny islet of Hobthrush, but that is not very secluded. Others say he went to the cave that is now called St Cuthbert's Cave, where we spent a lovely time in the sun having our lunch. Wherever he did spend time it still wasn't remote enough, so he asked permission to reside on a small island a few miles off the coast not far from Lindisfarne, called Inner Farne. No one lived on this island as it was reputedly inhabited by evil spirits; however this didn't deter Cuthbert as he arrived armed with the *sword of the Spirit, the word of God*, and the evil spirits were repulsed. Here he built for himself a small but happy cell and lived in contemplative isolation.

Unfortunately for Cuthbert, his solitary life of praying for the glory of God and fighting the forces of evil was not to last. The king himself came to Inner Farne to beg Cuthbert to take up the Bishopric of York. It is said he agreed *with a heavy heart*, and he was consecrated in York in 685. For just two years he worked with great zeal, travelling all over his diocese, but by 687 he knew he was dying. Perhaps the constant fasting and all-night praying and endless travelling and healing the sick were simply too much for one man, and so he resigned the bishopric and begged to return to Inner Farne.

Bede relates Cuthbert's final days, told to him by Herefrid, who was with Cuthbert to the end. Cuthbert returned to Inner Farne just after Christmas 686, living alone in his tiny cell, but it was usual for the monks to go out to visit him regularly. On one visit Herefrid found him very sick, and related to Bede that Cuthbert gave him some final deathbed instructions. He told him where his body should be buried on Inner Farne, as well as the linen cloak that he should be wrapped in – a gift from a great friend of his, the Abbess Verca – that he'd saved for exactly that reason. Herefrid, who had been on the point of leaving the island, begged to be allowed to stay, but Cuthbert refused and told him to return at the 'right time'. According to Bede, a storm then raged for five days before the distraught monks could return. When they did they found a very weak Cuthbert waiting for them to come back. In all that time his only available provisions had been five onions, and only one of them had been nibbled at, nothing more. He was near death, and even though he knew of Cuthbert's wish to remain on Inner Farne, Herefrid was anxious for him to be amongst them all and asked permission to transport his body back to Lindisfarne. Cuthbert remonstrated that many a bad person could come to seek sanctuary by his body, and therefore could cause problems for the monastery. Herefrid said he was happy to have such problems if it meant Cuthbert would be near them, so Cuthbert agreed and when he died on 20th March 687, he was taken back to Lindisfarne and buried in the Church of St Peter.

There were a few things left to do on our last afternoon on the Holy Island, and therefore our last afternoon of the Way, and one was to go to the heritage centre. It was exceptionally good – especially the film about the Viking raids. What a bloodthirsty lot they were! But truly fascinating were the electronic pages from the fabulous Lindisfarne Gospels. Brother Eadfrith created the original. It is the four gospels of the Bible written and painted on parchment of the finest quality. This illuminated book was carried with Cuthbert on his journey following his death to save this, too, from the hands of the Vikings. The original is now safely in the British Library, but here one can turn reproductions of its pages on a screen, and enjoy the beauty of such a wonderful work of art.

So, steeped in the history of the Holy Island, it was time for a walk along the water's edge at low tide, to appreciate the peacefulness and charm of being here. We walked to Hobthrush island and over to the cross sitting on the highest point of the small mound of land. A man was sitting on the far side with his Primus stove, boiling water and cooking the cockles stuck on the wet rocks before popping them into his mouth. He grinned at me and offered me one, but I declined. I wandered around the small island, which took about five minutes, before going back to the parish church where I stepped inside. Just by the door is a life-sized carving, in dark wood, of Cuthbert's coffin. It is borne by six monks, as with their heavy burden and bowed heads they bring him home into the body of the church.

It is a lovely way to finish. Lindisfarne is a serene end to a most glorious walk across the high reaches of northern Britain. Looking back from the threshold of the church I saw, over the water, the hills on the mainland dusted white by a new fall of snow. Brrr – time to get going.

5

St Hilda, Abbess of Whitby

North Yorkshire
7th century
Sixty-five kilometres
Maps: OS Explorer 26, 27

I think I would have been rather in awe of St Hilda, if not downright afraid of her. She sounds as though she was a formidable woman, but she was successful, and as a woman that was pretty rare, especially in medieval times. Nonetheless, I would have spent a lot of my time keeping out of her way if I had been part of her double monastery at Whitby. On the other hand, she was sought out by kings and bishops for her wisdom and advice.

It is a little bit sad that Whitby is better known nowadays for its association with Bram Stoker and *Dracula* and the subsequent black-clad goths than for the enormously important synod that took place here some 1,500 years ago in 664. Here the future of the Church in England was decided, and the future was with Europe.

It's not surprising Hilda was a tough nut. Her world was one of turmoil. Northumbria was constantly at war. She was born, according to the Venerable Bede in his *Ecclesiastical History*, in 614, the daughter of Hereric, a nephew of the king, but Hereric died soon after her birth. As a result, Hilda was raised as a ward of the king's court, where it is presumed she came under the influence of the king's second wife Æthelburg, the Christian Princess of Kent. Kent, of course, had been Christianised by St Augustine a few years before, and as part of her marriage negotiations Æthelburg had been allowed to bring with her the chaplain Paulinus. He came not only to minister to the queen, but also to convert as many heathens as possible. He succeeded, and Hilda was christened at the same time as King Edwin, when she was thirteen. For the first thirty-odd years of her life she lived a secular life. We have no biographical details from that period, and it may have been that she was married and ran her own household. It would be unusual, certainly, for a woman of the royal household not to be married either for dynastic or treaty purposes.

However, at thirty-three she decided to retire from the secular life and join her widowed sister in the nunnery in Chelles in France. But the great Celtic churchman of Lindisfarne, Aidan, called her back to Northumbria. Giving her a small parcel of land, he asked her to set up a household of prayer near the mouth of the River Wear. She agreed, and stayed for only a very short while before Aidan asked her to move on to Hartlepool. There, on a peninsula overlooking the salt marshes of the Tees Estuary, he instructed her to lead a community of men and women, where she was introduced to the Rule of Columbanus, and trained in the Celtic manner by Aidan himself. The community must have thrived and her success been recognised, as in 657 she was asked to found the double monastery at Whitby. She had it built high on the cliff overlooking the sea and the mouth of the Esk River and the little settlement of Whitby. It would have been a wooden palisade with completely separate buildings for the men and women, whom she kept strictly apart, except when at prayer in the church. She built up a library, a rarity in those days. She was an avid teacher and eager for her nuns and monks to study the holy books and know the word of God. Whitby became famous for its learning (at least five bishops were trained by Hilda), and many people from kings to paupers to churchmen came to seek her advice and wisdom. She was so beloved that according to Bede's writings of her, she was often called 'Mother'.

Whitby was famous throughout the country and growing in size and prestige, and in 664 King Oswiu, brother to Eanfrith and Oswald (and king after Oswald), came to Hilda's monastery to host a very important meeting. I have described already the synod at Whitby, but imagine how magnificent it must have been, and how amazingly important to be the hostess to a gathering of such magnitude. Whitby was the foremost centre of holiness and learning and nowhere else would do.

Before I set one foot on St Hilda's Way I had to go immediately to the abbey. I drove towards Whitby down the A171, over the northern edge of the Yorkshire Moors, and the sight I beheld as I came over the last hill on the way down to the town was stunning, and would have stopped me in my tracks if I hadn't been travelling in a line of traffic. Soon the traffic had to stop for some roadworks, and I was delighted to have the chance to simply sit and gaze at the view. I could see the shimmering sea through the ruined ribs of the abbey. It stands high and proud on the headland, overlooking the town to the south of the river's mouth. The tiny port below is overshadowed by the size and majesty of the Norman abbey. Nothing of the superstructure of the original buildings has survived. It was a long time ago, but more pertinently the place was absolutely ravaged by the Vikings, and on several occasions. When the Normans arrived they rebuilt the abbey in their own style, and that is what we see ruined today. It is marvellous. I took the excellent audio tour provided by English Heritage with me as, later, I walked slowly around the abbey, and listened to monks and nuns, and Cædmon the poet, talk of Hilda and their times. It is definitely worth listening to, and getting in the mood, before the walk itself.

The whole area is so delightful that any walk here is really wonderful. Mine started in Hinderwell. I was using the guide written by Nancy and John Eckersley, who created the Way over fields and by joining up well-known public paths and rights of way. Hinderwell is the start because of St Hilda's Well: the name 'Hinderwell' derives from it. I took the bus from Whitby and hopped off next to the church and found the well in the graveyard – not so much a well as a small bubbling spring. Tradition says that St Hilda stopped here to drink from this spring on her way north, and afterwards she was *wondrously invigorated*. A kind parishioner restored the well in 1912. From St Hilda's Church the public footpath leads off between the houses of the village, winding about on a narrow, walled path which sometimes made me feel as though I was walking in someone's front garden. Before too long it opened out at a farm and then led down into the sharp valley below. It's very inviting. Below me was a bank of trees. Lovely and thick, full of leaf and bright green, nestled in the cleft formed by the now-tiny stream that runs through it. Where once there may have been a raging torrent is now Dale Beck, only a muddy stream.

But I was soon out of the trees and crossing an open field, over Barrowby Dale. I stopped to gaze about me, looking over to the coast and the glittering sea, and back towards the village of Hinderwell. The path continues up before turning left and along the side of the hill, through very overgrown paths, but still just about recognisable, until I came out by Low Barrowby farmhouse. So far on the walk I hadn't met any people, or animals. Suddenly two dogs raised an enormous racket, barking like crazy. I jumped out of my skin. It had been so quiet, with me in my usual dreamlike state that I adopt when I walk (which is one of the reasons I get lost so frequently). Anyway, I'm sure that pilgrims to Whitby coming this way, or the Whitby brothers going out to spread the word of God, would have had to cope with many dogs, but these were tiny; two very vocal but obviously lapdogs. The dogs were followed by a couple of young girls who took one look at me and decided I would offer no excitement at all, and shot past me. Following them was their grandmother, with whom I had a lovely chat.

But after a while it was time to walk on and find my path, so I scrambled around in the field and eventually found the stile. It was covered with tall nettles, so taking my time to beat them down, I jumped over and landed in very, very soft ground. I was high on the side of the moor, Barrowby Moor now, but it was a morass and, moreover, the cows often walked through here. With enormous care I sought and tested each tussock, hoping my weight would be held, and luckily I managed without too much problem.

I was enjoying myself walking through the fields, watching the sky turning progressively darker, and then a few drops fell, hitting me in the face very gently. I stopped to don my waterproofs, just in time, when a torrent hit me from the heavens, but I was well protected and quite content to carry on. Still on a public footpath, I saw it go off into the distance, but my guide told me to veer off right, on a farmer's track, and walk up to a lane. Here I strode out, enjoying not having to watch where I put my feet but glancing up, now and again with a face full of rain, to watch the clouds billowing over my head. Perhaps they took up too much of my attention and I missed a vital path, or perhaps it was because, just by that particular gate – having tramped through a few miles of boggy moorland – were a group of cows. Not just any cows, but huge beasts, and more importantly, their calves. They stood looking at me with lowered heads, watching as I came closer. They didn't look like they were thinking of moving out of my way. They started, instead, to shift into a defensive ring around the little ones – their bums pushing up against the gate I thought I needed. *Never mind*, I said to myself, *I'm sure it's fine and I'm sure the cows don't need to be disturbed*.

So I trudged on, now on Roxby Low Moor, still in the rain, and eventually came down to the A171. Oh my goodness, do people move fast on this road. I must have done too, when I was driving along it, but walking it was not pleasant. If I had gone through that 'cow gate' my walk would have still brought me to the road, but further down. As it turned out I had at least a couple of kilometres, as opposed to a few hundred metres, to endure. In the rain, the thundering lorries threw up monstrous spray and I was fairly running on the grass verge at the side of the road. Then, phew – I found a parking place with a tea stall. Off the road I fled gratefully and, to steady my nerves, had a cup of welcome tea. It was only a shortish walk down to meet the bus back to Whitby. Wet and chilly, I think I steamed on the bus.

But what a difference a day makes – the next stretch of the walk was open moorland. What a shame it would have been to not be able to enjoy the views. But I had a perfect day; the sort of day that would have had pilgrims and brothers singing with the joy of being alive. The sun shone, the breeze was cool and gentle, and the birds were singing.

I started by Scaling Dam; dropped by the bus at the same stop as the day before. Oh, so different. The path started in the car park of the sailing clubhouse and went through a bit of a wood to the edge, then left to skirt around the bottom of the dam's perimeter on Boghouse Lane and cross over Boghouse Beck. I had the dam on my left, and stretching away to my right were Easington High Moor and Bella Dale Slack. The path was pretty easy to follow initially, but my guide showed me I had to come off the footpath and join a bridleway. I couldn't see it. The moor rises and dips and I couldn't make out where the new path lay between the heathers. Luckily my phone map gave me my precise, pinpoint position, so I walked it blind, until I literally stood in the right spot and could just make it out. It was enough to walk on, and very soon it became a double-track path. Oh, how glorious it was. The sky was huge and the red grouse all around me were clacking. The meadow pipits were 'pipiting' at me, and I was delighted to spot a snipe as it flew away from my noisy approach. The skylarks are invariably with me on my walks and I do miss them when I can't hear them, but here they were plentiful. I kept an eye open for merlins that I believed could be about, but I saw no birds of prey.

I was slowly but surely walking up an incline, getting gradually higher and higher. Purple heather and lots of clusters of small white flowers surrounded me. A few sheep wandered about, looking up from their grazing when they heard me and without haste moving off. Sadly I came across the bloated body of a dead sheep lying on the track. I could see no reason for its death, but I was perturbed that in its swollen state it could be near to exploding. I gave it a fairly wide berth and moved on quite quickly. So often as I followed the track, a grouse or several would fly up from under my feet, clacking madly, then fly off awkwardly to cover further away. The shooting season was fast approaching, when their numbers would be thinned considerably. I was passing several grouse butts all over the moor.

As the ground rose under my feet I was coming to the highest point of the whole walk at Beacon Hill, called Danby Beacon. For four hundred years a beacon has stood here in readiness as part of the defence of the kingdom. In the 1600s especially, England lived under the constant menace of invasion. One was, of course, the Armada, but over the centuries there have been numerous rumours and threats. The Danby Beacon was one of a line of beacons, usually twenty miles or so apart, that were lit at the first sign of an enemy fleet. The message would then be sent, via the lit fires, to ready the forces. The old wooden beacon rotted away, so now there stands a steel-and-bronze one – bronze, apparently, in a nod to the Bronze Age burial mound that forms part of the hill.

As I looked out over the view from the beacon, I was joined by half a dozen or so runners who had come up the steep hill behind me and were off to my left within a moment – I think they were on their way to Whitby some fifteen-odd miles away. I sedately ambled off down towards the Moors Visitor Centre. The guide takes the path over the top of the centre, staying high before dropping down to the village of Danby, but I wanted to pop in and have a look, so I deviated a little. The road down was so steep I was doing pigeon steps to preserve my knees, and coming up were two girls pushing massively laden bikes. The first one stopped, breathing heavily, and asked between gasps how much further up to the top. I could assure her it wasn't too far. It is very steep here, but it is short, and within a couple of minutes I was in the centre.

The Eckersley guide has some options for walking in the footsteps of Hilda. There is the straightforward walk through, and then there are loops to take in the several churches that are connected with the saint. One of these is St Hilda's Church. I decided to walk there before going on. It is a few kilometres out of Danby; in fact I thought it strangely remote from the village. I wondered if the village had been moved when the railway line was built so that it would be closer to that, but it did not look as though there was ever much around the church. Surrounded by its graveyard and enormous yews, it looked secluded and holy.

One of the first things I saw as I got inside was a large stained-glass window that depicted St Hilda with the main characters involved with the Whitby Synod. One was of the Venerable Bede, who wrote it all down for us; then Cædmon the poet, to whom Hilda taught the words of God and who made them into songs for his glory; next was St Wilfrid, the victor of the fierce debate; and lastly Archbishop Colmán, who lost the argument and retired to Ireland to live out his life worshipping, as he always had, in the Celtic fashion.

The next stage of the walk is very well signposted. St Hilda's Way now walks in the footsteps of the Esk Valley Way. With a leaping salmon as its icon, I more or less put away my guidebook and just walked where others had walked before me. The walk out of Danby goes via the Moors Visitor Centre again, and along the flat of the valley through a couple of fields before joining an old bridleway that took me back onto the edge of Lealholm Moor. I was on a good tarred road, very narrow and quite busy, but with no hedges or fences I could just step off onto the grass. I was enjoying the scudding clouds and the wind in my face, looking out over the whole of the Esk Valley. What a view. Amazing. Sunlight would pop out from the clouds every now and again and illuminate a few fields across the valley, and sometimes race across the land before being 'eaten up' by the clouds again. Magnificent. I watched a couple of RAF planes too, circling and roaring. Three times they flew directly over my head at tremendous speed, then turned just over me so I had the full benefit of the afterburners' deafening roar. It was fun, albeit loud.

A couple of hours later the route dropped down into the village of Lealholm, past the station and over the railway bridge, turning right before the river. The route now runs between the river and the railway, mostly right on the riverbank for a while, then crossing to the south side all the way to Glaisdale. This is a steep little village. It used to be an ironstone mining centre but now it's all about tourism. Just outside the village is the Beggar's Bridge. I read a sign which stated that it was built by a Mr Tom Ferries in 1619. The story goes that he, the son of a moorland farmer, was in love with Agnes, the daughter of a well-to-do gentleman who did not consider Tom a suitable match for his Agnes. Tom resolved to go away and make his fortune, but wished for a last kiss from his beloved. Unfortunately the river was in flood and they couldn't reach each other, but only stare and bid goodbye. Off he went to join Francis Drake's navy, and came home a very rich man. Agnes and he married, and he built the bridge in memory of his lost kiss.

Walking out of Glaisdale on the south side of the river, the path goes through the East Arnecliff Wood. This is a big stretch of woods, which at times winds up the hill and down, on stone slabs known as *trods*, laid down in medieval times to aid walkers in the mud and the muck. The trees looked very ancient indeed. Large alders, oaks, birch and hazel I could identify, but there were many others. The sunlight dappled through the branches and the breeze was twirling the leaves. I met no one until I got to Egton Bridge, where I turned off to visit the church.

In this tiny village, tucked away from the rest of the world in a deep valley of the North Yorkshire Moors – far, far away from the centre of the ruling world in London – recusant Catholics still worshipped, although in hiding. As I walked into Egton Bridge and turned left, I spotted the Church of St Hedda in front of me. Here are held the relics of the martyr Nicholas Postgate. Unfortunately for Postgate and all Roman Catholics at this time, the religion had been banned on pain of death following Henry VIII's break with the pope in Rome. Anyone caught worshipping in the Roman fashion was to be killed. Postgate was executed in 1679 after his arrest in the middle of a baptism he was performing in Little Beck near Whitby, but it's here at Egton Bridge that he was born in 1596 and spent most of his life. In 1621 he went to study at Douay College in France, and by 1628 he had taken his final priestly vows. He was sent back to Britain to preach the Catholic religion in secret and set up shop in nearby Ugthorpe until 1678, when he was betrayed to the authorities and arrested. He was caught up in the fervent sweep following Titus Oates' concocted conspiracy of a Popish Plot to replace King Charles II with a Catholic king. Postgate was hanged, drawn and quartered, with one of his hands being sent to his old college in Douay. The rest of his relics are now housed in St Hedda's. He was beatified in 1987 by Pope John Paul II, along with eighty-five other English Catholic martyrs, for being a recusant Catholic priest.

The path continues on from near St Hedda's and follows a bridleway from Egton Bridge to Grosmont – a nice, easy path with scattered sheep. It turned out to be a toll road, but there was no toll exacted from walkers so I was fine to continue on my way, free from any payment. (I think this sign ceased to be relevant a very long time ago.) I was looking forward to getting to Grosmont as I was hoping to catch sight of one of the rather wonderful steam trains that chug noisily between here and Whitby. Grosmont village was originally called Tunnel. Just Tunnel. It was created during the 1830s in the manic rush of the Industrial Revolution because of the iron mining in the district.

However, the modern name comes from a priory in the area before it was closed down during the Dissolution. The priory was of the Grandmontine order, and I suppose the name 'Grosmont' has come from that. Sadly, though, my timings for the train were all wrong, and even though further down the track I heard the delightful *puff-puff* and *hoot-hoot* of a steam engine, I didn't see anything through the trees. I was interested to read that the station here in Grosmont was built in 1836, the same year as the somewhat larger station at London Bridge was opened. It was initially a horse-drawn route to Whitby, but the trains arrived a few years later. The normal Whitby train stops here too, for you who want to pause here and get a ride into town. I walked past the village in the thick trees and made my way up farm tracks and small lanes and the edges of fields for the five kilometres or so to the next village of Sleights – through a couple of farmyards too, which were mostly empty but for the geese in one. Alarmed at my approach, they created quite a hullabaloo, like the guard-geese who protected Rome from the barbarians. They followed me for a bit, cackling away, then when they realised I wasn't going to feed them they lost interest and wandered off!

The final stretch into Whitby starts in Sleights, where I had decided to begin a new day's walking. It was an evil-weather day, but we have them, and it just meant that my first view of the abbey from here was obscured by wind and rain.

The walk from Sleights into Whitby is just over seven kilometres, so a short walk from the station. The path leads one almost immediately away from the village and through farms, walking through fields and over stiles. Most of the time I was wading through long (and very wet) grass, but as the route neared the outskirts of town the houses became less farmhouse-y and more like smart and expensive suburban dwellings. At Buskey House farmhouse, the path leaves the fields and joins a small road that leads into Sneaton village and then crosses over one of the main routes into Whitby. The traffic is a bit scary, but running over (with care), I found on the other side another church named in honour of St Hilda. This one probably had closer ties to the abbey by its sheer proximity; it is only a short walk between the two of them. This St Hilda's was cold and damp. To reach the front porch I had to open a small, rickety, rusty gate that swung open with an ominous squeak. I thought it was exactly the sort of noise that on a dark and stormy night would be very spooky. All I needed was a hooting owl to give me the full range of spookiness. The path up to the church door was laid with slabs of the local stone. These were wet and were lethally slippery. I negotiated the path with great care, went inside and walked around for a while.

With only a few more kilometres to go from here I walked back out to the road, clutching the rail to keep upright, to the small footpath next door to the graveyard. The path here is called the Monk's Trod, as monks would have used it continuously. The trod is made of the same stone slabs as near Glaisdale, but thankfully not as slippery as the path to St Hilda's. The route goes down through the ancient woods and over very small streams or becks, almost right into the suburbs of Whitby itself. I had such a strong feeling of other feet that had been here before, and for the first time on this walk I encountered a fellow walker nearby. He was wearing jeans that he confessed to me were falling off with the weight of all the rainwater he been subjected to! It had carried on raining the whole way from Sleights.

The path pops out close to town and joins a cycle route called the Cinder Trail. This is a newly created cycle path along the old disused railway track. It's a great walk and cycle path. It crosses the river on a high bridge and then carries down to the old cargo station tracks right by the harbour at Whitby. This is now the main car park in the centre of town, near to the main street and supermarkets and lovely places to sit and enjoy people-watching over a hot drink or an ice cream, depending on your tastes.

I walked (after my cup of tea) through the car park and up through the town, past all the tourists and over the swing bridge. Here are the ancient, wiggly streets of old Whitby, with cobblestones and hideaway entrances to houses. A sweep at the end of one of the larger streets ends with the steps up to the great abbey above. There are 199 steps up to the Church of St Mary and then the abbey on the clifftop. This was the monks' route into town. The Normans built St Mary's Church, just below the abbey, originally in 1110. Now it is a starkly Anglican 18th-century church with box pews and a remarkable three-tiered pulpit. It is definitely worth stopping by to see this magnificent Protestant church. Cædmon, the poet and favourite of St Hilda, has a cross dedicated to him in the graveyard. In his spine-chilling novel, Bram Stoker brought Dracula here and made him creep about, looking evil; hence there is now an annual invasion of goths for the Whitby Goth Weekend.

Cholmley House, which was built by the Cholmley family in 1672, lies between St Mary's and the abbey. The family owned the abbey before English Heritage took over both it and the house in 1936. The house is now a visitors' centre dedicated to the finds discovered on the site, and its history too. I walked in and had a look at some of the archaeological artefacts including an amazing Anglo-Saxon comb made out of animal bone with runic symbols, and some incredible writing tools too. I didn't linger long as I was powerfully drawn back to the great, brooding abbey standing proud ahead of me.

I walked out over to where the high altar would have been and gazed about me at the remains of a once-mighty and bustling community of nuns and monks. Hilda stayed here until almost the end of her life in 680, but in that last year the indefatigable lady set up yet another monastery a few kilometres away in Hackness. It was there that the bells rang in sorrow at the moment of her death on the 17th November. She is often shown in pictures with ammonites at her feet to represent the pit of snakes she is said to have petrified – these explained the fossilised ammonites on the beach below the abbey, and the locals say that birds dip their wings in honour of the Lady Hilda as they fly overhead.

Standing in the wind next to the great building I could look north over the town below, east to the great moors and hills, and west over the twinkling sea that eventually brought such ruin to the abbey with the arrival of the Vikings, but it all survived until the fateful Dissolution. Hilda is said to have accepted the king's ruling during the synod to worship in the ways from Rome, but I feel she would have been very forceful in her condemnation of the destruction of her beloved monastery to turn the Church to the Protestant way. I'm glad she never saw it.

6

The Laughing Bishop

11th century
Sussex
50 km
Maps: OS Explorer OL8, OL10

Written by Richard of Chichester:
Thanks be to thee, my Lord Jesus Christ, for all the benefits thou hast given me, for all the pains and insults thou hast borne for me. Oh, merciful redeemer, friend and brother, may I know thee more clearly, love thee more dearly and follow thee more nearly, day by day.

St Richard was born in a time when Crown and Church were constantly vying for power; actually, I suppose it was ever thus. It may have been simply a personality clash in his situation, but with on one side an all-powerful king, and on the other an all-powerful churchman, Richard was just a pawn in their power games and had little say in how events affected him. This was many centuries before the Crown made its 'demands' into its 'absolute commands' with Henry VIII.

Richard of Chichester was born Richard Backindine in 1197, and was called formally Richard de Wych from Droitwych (now Droitwich), Worcestershire. He died at the age of fifty-six in Dover on the 3rd of April 1253, having been bishop for only eight years. It took a while before he was recognised as a saint, despite the odd miracle during his lifetime. He was not of particularly noble birth but his yeoman father did own his own land, and they seem to have been a fairly prosperous family. Unfortunately for Richard, his elder brother and their sister, both parents died when they were very young, and that prosperity was whittled away by overseers until they were on the point of bankruptcy. Finally it was time for the elder brother to take control of the estate, and Richard apparently toiled hard to rebuild and restore the property. His brother was not as successful a farmer as Richard and so he generously offered him the entire property, but that and the prospect of an advantageous marriage wasn't enough to keep Richard at home. He had a yearning for study.

He spent several years at Oxford before going on to Paris and Bologna where he gained a degree in canon law. On his return to Oxford in 1235 he was made chancellor of the university. While at Oxford during his earlier studies he had been tutored by, and made a friend of, the highly respected (but perhaps not very popular) Edmund of Abingdon. Edmund had himself studied at Oxford and Paris, and was appointed Archbishop of Canterbury by Pope Gregory IX in 1233. Edmund really wasn't the favourite choice; the chapter at Canterbury had suggested three other candidates that the pope had rejected, and Edmund came in only as an alternative.

Edmund and Richard had similar views on reforms in the church in England and independence from Rome, as well as the strength of secular powers meddling in church matters, namely King Henry III. Edmund was a good judge of ability and appointed Richard as his chancellor in Canterbury. In his early dealings with King Henry on his elevation, Edmund had incurred his dislike. Amazingly, he had the audacity to order the king to dismiss his favourite councillors on pain of excommunication, which the king did do, but he didn't like it at all. Edmund also managed to upset a lot of other people with his rigid stances on monastic observance and good discipline, and in 1237 he set out for Rome to plead his position, and took Richard with him. Accounts of Edmund's life vary here. He did die in 1240, in the Cistercian monastery in Pontigny, but some accounts say he was in exile here because he'd made so many enemies, while others say he died on his return from his embassy to Rome. Whichever is right, the accounts do mention Richard was with him still when he died.

At this point Richard decided to become a priest and spent the next few years with the Dominicans in Orleans in France, studying theology. He was ordained in 1242, whereupon he immediately returned to England to take up as parish priest in Charing and Deal. The Archbishop of Canterbury, Boniface of Savoy, had other ideas and reappointed him chancellor in Canterbury instead.

In 1244 the incumbent Bishop of Chichester died, and the chapter there elected Richard as their new bishop. King Henry III was furious (he disliked Richard as much as he had Edmund) and refused to accept the appointment. Boniface, on the other side, refused to accept Henry's selection of Bishop Richard Passelew. Impasse. So they appealed to the pope in Rome, Innocent IV. The pope confirmed Richard of Chichester and the king promptly confiscated the see and lands (and revenues) of Chichester Cathedral, and for two years Richard was a wandering bishop. He was forbidden to live in Chichester and the king forbade anyone from giving him food or shelter. One of Richard's greatest friends was the priest of the nearby parish of Tarring, Simon. Simon ignored the king's orders and for two years Richard stayed with him in Tarring, walking to Chichester to minister to his people.

The village of Tarring is now part of Worthing in West Sussex, only a very short walking distance to the seashore. The parish church is St Andrew's and the first mention of it was in very early 939 AD, when King Æthelstan gifted the manor of Tarring to the see at Canterbury. The 1086 Domesday Book also mentions Tarring, which it notes had forty-one inhabitants. There are a few more now, although its larger neighbour has swallowed up the original village. The original high street still exists, along with a few lovely and ancient-looking pubs. St Andrew's was once a large and prosperous parish but now has been reduced in size and influence, and is from the outside a pretty normal English church. Surrounded by the usual yew trees and cherry blossom, the gravestones are old, moss-covered and mostly illegible, tilting gently earthwards at odd angles from one another in the uneven ground. The website on the history of the church tells that in 1561 drinking sessions were held in the church to raise funds for its upkeep; an exercise unlikely to be replicated today. Even though I couldn't get in (it's only open a couple of days a week, for a few hours), It said too that St Andrew's has spectacular mosaics of the twelve apostles covering the walls of the nave, created by William Butterfield based on the mosaics in Ravenna. I'm sure they're worth a visit when possible.

My walk started when, sadly, the weather was not so fabulous. It poured with rain and the wind was so blustery and gusty it destroyed my umbrella and left me with no defence against the soaking skies. There is no known pilgrimage route, nor an organised one, from here to Chichester, but for two years or more Richard would have walked to his cathedral. I am supposing his route would have been the most direct as the crow flies, from Point A at Tarring to Point B at Chichester. This would have taken him down the A259, through East Preston and Wick to Littlehampton, before heading due north-west up to Chichester. This was not a route that held great appeal for me to walk now, along the roads. I reckon Richard would be most surprised to see the route now, changed beyond all recognition. So I decided to take a different path, and following in Richard's general direction, I walked in his footsteps from the door of St Andrew's to the door of Chichester Cathedral, through the gorgeous countryside he would have known so well.

I started from the church lychgate, down the pretty, deserted urban streets of Worthing town to the Esplanade and turned right. I actually enjoyed walking, unusually for me, through the streets, staring at the neat gardens and clipped lawns before getting down to the seashore. It was a howling, stormy day, but quite beautiful, and following the West Parade I stayed by the sea, walking past Goring-by-Sea and through on to Ferring. It was wonderfully refreshing. The clouds were billowing ahead and I was greeted by lots of dog walkers who were also braving the elements. Of course in the town's precincts, I was on easy pathways, but as the town faded behind me, the path took me through grassy parks and car parks, over the shingle and onto a broad grass strip that separates the houses from the worst the sea can throw at them. I noted that several, in fact most, of the houses had flood barriers in the walls of their gardens. They are generally at least a hundred metres from the shingle, but I suppose, on a high tide with a pushing wind, the water could be whipped into a high frenzy.

On I stepped, across the shingle and paths, and eventually the dog walkers thinned out and there was, madly, just me. It's been a long time since I've had the opportunity to walk down by the sea, and the wind whipping through my hair was a wonderful feeling. The effort of walking on shingle pleased me too, in a silly way, as the walk so far had been much too easy and wonderful, so slipping and sliding about on the rounded and wet sea stones was semi-hard work – all the better to remind me that this was a walk and not a Sunday afternoon stroll down on the beach! However, I think the drenching rain would have dissuaded me from venturing out if it had simply been a Sunday stroll. I watched the cargo ships sliding down through the English Channel in the distant murk. This whole coast must have been rife with smuggling and endless trips over to France; it is, after all, very close by. On an information board in town I read a story of Worthing in the early 1800s. A huge gang of two to three hundred men was caught smuggling and chased by the excise men, who managed to shoot and kill a few of them. That success was apparently, and surprisingly, the end of that source of income.

This whole coast, though, has always been a favourite summer holiday destination for the wealthy and fashionable from London. The railway came down here in 1845, opening the area up to even more visitors with such easy travel. One might say things haven't changed much as Worthing appears to be still very fashionable and popular. The whole way along the coast is built up. I saw barely a foot of land that was not built on, all the way from Worthing to Littlehampton. Some were archetypal 1950s English seaside houses, but some were mega-mansions, and then there were the Art Deco-style new houses painted white, with enormous glass windows. I felt a bit voyeuristic staring in, but it was so fascinating I couldn't help myself. They were all empty as far as I could see. Since it was such a dark day thanks to the storm, anyone inside would have needed lights on, but every house was dark and cold-looking. I thought to myself that although the view of the sea from those vast panes of glass would have been magnificent, they would be constantly smeared with salt from the waves, and hence a nightmare to clean… what a prosaic thought!

The path is, of course, pretty easy to follow – just stick by the sea – but at one stage I was forced to walk off the beach by the Bluebird Café. I was thinking of popping in for a nice cuppa, but then saw through the window that it was packed inside. Not a table looked free and I was soaking wet, which meant I would drip terribly, so I didn't think I'd be very welcome amongst them. I did manage a sit-down in a café in Littlehampton a few kilometres further on. Initially I wanted to just have a rest and some respite from the weather, but it turned out to be the end of my day. Unlike St Richard, who I'm sure was made of sterner stuff than I, in no great hurry, I gave up for the day in favour of the better weather promised for the next day.

The weatherman kept his promise and the following day was far nicer when I picked up the trail again in Littlehampton. The sun was shining fitfully as I walked down by the Arun River. It was moored with some lovely-looking boats, and also the occasional one that had seen better days; sunk into the sludgy mud and looking like ghosts.

At the mouth of the river I entered the West Beach Local Nature Reserve on a path that took me through the marram grass into the dunes. The reserve was set up in 1995, and is a Site of Special Scientific Interest. It covers the dunes, the shoreline, the shingle and sand flats of course, and all the small creatures that live here. It was wonderful to be high above the beach and enjoy a spectacular view over the sea. Rock pipits flying out of the grasses surrounded me, and I spotted what looked to be a small weasel which dashed madly between the tussocks, but I'm not sure that dunes are their preferred habitat. The dunes themselves looked in good health. Within the reserve, or rather between the reserve and the Littlehampton Golf Course that runs alongside it, lie the ruins of Littlehampton Fort. Almost overgrown, it was built in response to the putative threat of invasion by the French during the see-sawing of Anglo-French relations in the early 19th century. The threats came to nothing and the tower was demolished in 1891 and simply forgotten about. During the Second World War, Littlehampton was a centre for air and sea rescue patrols but the fort wasn't used even then. West Beach was, though, as it was used to practise landings in preparation for D-Day.

The beach stretches on. It was mostly empty but occasionally a birdwatcher would appear from amongst the dunes with binoculars dangling around their neck, and thick warm jackets always in green to blend with the background. I'm always impressed with birdwatchers for their patience and ability to sit still in cold and wet situations. I'd freeze even in temperate weather, let alone the cold and wet…

A few miles on, it was time to come off the beach. Ever since ..
West Beach Nature Reserve the beach had been free of any buildings.
The public footpath runs mainly on the shingle but sometimes it veers
down very small and quiet lanes, and through car parks, and next to
(sadly closed) ice-cream and tea stalls. It had all been lovely and quiet,
still quite early and no one was out and about as yet. But as I came
around a corner, I saw a woman standing staring at the bushes on the
side of the narrow lane. She looked slightly strange, standing there
looking intently into the bushes. She was concentrating very hard, but
I could see nothing. I said hello and she jumped around in fright. All of
a sudden, her dog shot out of the undergrowth: a beautifully groomed
miniature collie called Bella. She was far too gorgeous and clean to be
outside at all.

Around the next corner I walked past some badly destroyed sea wall
that reminded me again of the power of the sea. Soon I got off the little
lane and back on the beach, but it wasn't long after that I ran out of
beach – the nearer I got to Bognor Regis, the harder it was to simply
follow a path westwards. I had to head slightly away from the sea, and
I was soon lost in the small roads and houses of Felpham. Eventually, I
found myself being taken into the centre of Bognor Regis itself, and past
the vast complex that is the Butlins holiday resort. It was huge. So many
signs – to car parks for long stays, car parks for day trippers, deliveries,
swimming pool, and goodness only knows what else. A magnificent
centre for simply having fun for all the family. It was pretty empty as
far as I could see, but since it was neither holiday season nor even very
warm, I'm not surprised. I knew nothing of Bognor Regis, but it's a
typical English coastal holiday town. Several shops selling buckets and
spades, and lots of kiosks waiting for the sunshine and punters to buy
their ice creams and lollies. It looked cared for and a nice, gentle place
to live – I loved the seafront. It hadn't been cluttered up, and the sea
looked stunning now the sun had appeared again, calm and peaceful. It
was all beach walking from here for about five kilometres. It was mostly

wide open and flat, but sometimes it narrowed and became quite steep and I was forced onto the sea wall. In one section the wall has been so beaten by the sea that it's impassable, but luckily it was possible to jump back onto the shingle without too much of a problem. Otherwise, it's pretty plain sailing until Pagham.

I thought all would be happy and pretty, and everyone would be joyful with the gorgeousness of his or her surroundings. But I was wrong! I had wondered to myself about the steepness of the beach here, and thought it odd that some of the boats were pulled up so high, sitting on small cliffs without so much as a run down to the water. Maybe, I pondered, they were just there temporarily and hence there wasn't much reason to organise things properly. As I said, I was wrong. Over the last few years, an enormous spit has been growing in front of Pagham Harbour. This has caused major changes to the beach and is even now threatening the houses along this stretch. The official website for the Pagham Flood Defence Steering Group has produced a fascinating bit of film showing what is happening to their beach and community – it's worth a look. I was oblivious to this when I scrambled over the lip of loose shingle and ended up in the Pagham Beach Café. The spit is a serious threat to this part of the coastline and the locals are desperate to do something about it. I heard all about it over a drink in the café. Not an easy problem to sort out, but they are trying.

Pagham was where I needed to come away from the shore and start heading up to Chichester. After passing time with the locals in the café, I took out my OS map and found the start of the public footpath that wound around the wetland area of Pagham Lagoon, and through the mobile home park into the village of Pagham. I popped into the church there, but didn't stay as there were masses of people organising flowers and being very busy. Still, it was a nice village church. The map did show that is probably a better walk, carrying on around the lagoon rather than come into the village, as it was the natural way to walk to Pagham Wall.

Pagham Wall is part of the old harbour, from when the village was right by the water. Now it has silted up and the water is about a kilometre away. But it is still wet, and the large stretch of wetland and mudflats has become a refuge, or stopover, for migrating birds. It was a glorious sight with the sun shining and clouds gently floating on the horizon. One white swan was diving; staying under so long I started to be slightly concerned. It came up for air and without a second's hesitation, dipped down again for more of whatever it was enjoying down there.

Soon it was time to take to the open fields and I tracked across a couple of them, watching out for the styles in the hedges on the other side. It was clear and lovely and easy to follow, until one turning, which my map indicated, never happened. The field was full of huge cows. Is it just me or are cows getting bigger? I never thought they'd be a worry but these were just too interested, which caused me to walk on and not search about for a non-existent footpath. Anyway, I had an idea that the infamous churchman and firebrand St Wilfrid was in this area during his exile, and I had an inkling to follow this up. So I followed footpaths, heading more towards the west, until I found myself in the tiny village of Selsey. Usually I can see the spire of the church in most villages I come into, it being the highest point, but I could see nothing here, so I asked a couple sitting in their car having a coffee from their thermos, and they pointed to behind me – there it was! It is the tiniest church and could have held no more than a dozen parishioners at the very best of times. Wilfrid must have put the fear of God in them, literally. I felt rather sorry for them, even several centuries since.

But enough of Wilfrid; I was walking with Richard, and Chichester was calling, so to speak, so I turned north. Much to my horror, there were no footpaths to follow. I was forced to walk along a couple of very fast roads with no pavements and difficult, grassy banks to walk on. I had to stand with my back pushed into the hedge, trying to avoid the nettles, to get out of the cars' way. So best not to go via Selsey. Eventually I got onto a golf course, which became my refuge, even if one needs to keep a weather eye out for flying balls. The footpath officially goes through the course and it is lovely and quiet after the roads. Getting nearer to the city, the path comes into the village of Hunston and from here on, it's a lovely, easy stroll down the Chichester Canal and into the suburbs, and I was inspired to walk with more of a spring in my step towards the great spire of the cathedral.

St Richard is not forgotten. There is a fine, full-sized statue of him outside the cathedral, in full view of the local populace. He was hard to miss. Nearby is one of the busiest bus stops in Chichester. Walking down the high street, I was dodging throngs of people going about their business, from schoolkids coming home, to working mums and dads rushing home from offices, and grannies and grandads shopping for supper. No different to the people who would have known Bishop Richard.

After two whole years of Richard walking between his friend Simon's home in Tarring to his cathedral in Chichester, the king relented. So it was that finally, in 1246, Richard could move in. It was not that the king relented; more that he was threatened with excommunication by the pope, so he finally handed over the bishopric. That meant, too, that he lost the revenue from the lands, which he had been taking for those two years. Richard was a simple man and not in need of the revenue for himself. He was an ascetic and reputedly wore a hair shirt, ate no meat and refused to eat off silver.

So Richard finally was in charge and he wasted no time in sorting out the morals of the clergy – priests mumbling during Mass were castigated, corrupt priests he treated without mercy, and even in his dealings with the king, still Henry III, he defied him. One story was of a priest who seduced a nun. The king asked for leniency for the seducer. Richard was having none of it and defrocked the man. A famous story also tells of a thief whom the townsfolk of Lewes strung up and hanged, having dragged him from the church. Richard demanded him cut down and buried properly in consecrated ground, since they had violated the right of sanctuary. His contemporaries held him up as the perfect bishop. He decreed that the sacraments should be given without payment, and that the clergy must be celibate and look like clergy – i.e. wear religious dress. But the laity too had orders. They needed to go to church on Sundays, and to know by heart the Creed, the Our Father and the Hail Mary prayers. The website in Richard's name refers to him ruling his clergy *as a master does his pupils* and his own household *as a father does his sons*, and says that Chichester Cathedral states that *in his lifetime he was known as the laughing bishop.*

In 1253 Richard was ordered by the pope to preach a holy Crusade to recover the lands occupied by the Saracens. Exhausted with all his austere living and hard work, he died on the 3rd of April, in the arms of his friends Simon of Tarring and his chaplain William, in Dover. His heart stayed in Dover but his body was brought back to Chichester and buried in the cathedral. Some nine years later in 1262, he was canonised by Pope Urban IV, after 'great miracles' were performed at his tomb.

As I entered the main door of the cathedral, a couple of volunteers moved forward with welcoming smiles, and asked if I'd been there before. "No," I said, "but I would love to have a blessing if it's at all possible." One looked sceptical while the other beamed with a great smile, and, touching my arm, asked me to wait while she shot off into the nether regions of the cathedral. I chatted to the other for a short while, but then Lizzy appeared. She explained she wasn't a dean but simply a reader so couldn't actually give me a blessing, but she could pray with me. I said that would be lovely. I explained to her about St Richard and we prayed for pilgrims and for my walks, and then we had a long chat about pilgrimages in general and the great route to Santiago, swapping stories of our experiences on the Camino.

The cathedral is lovely and light-filled, and obviously well loved by its people. I wandered around to find the shrine to Richard – a modern shrine, of course. The original one, that had been the focus of many pilgrims coming from afar, was destroyed on the orders of King Henry

VIII in his mass destruction of the Dissolution. It had been one of the most popular shrines, second only for some time to the shrine of St Thomas at Canterbury, but as with all the others was destroyed and the bones removed. A legend went that someone managed to steal them and salt them away. According to Richard's Wikipedia page, in 1987 the Abbey of La Lucerne in Normandy found part of a man's arm in a reliquary believed to be that of Richard. After an investigation into its story, it was offered to and accepted by the then-Bishop of Chichester in 1990. It was reburied with great ceremony below what is now the Altar of St Richard. Another relic, authenticated by the Vatican, was also sent to Chichester to honour their saint.

So I walked in the footsteps of, and learnt about, St Richard of Chichester and walked in the countryside he would have known so well, and I'm sure loved very much. He was loved, too, by his people. He is the patron saint of Sussex and his translated saint's day of 16th June is celebrated as Sussex Day. Perhaps more than all this, though, he left a poignant prayer that is even today sung in both the Anglican and Roman Catholic churches:

Day by day, dear Lord,
Of these three things I pray:
To see thee more clearly,
Love thee more dearly,
Follow thee more nearly,
Day by day.

These are the words he spoke on his deathbed all those centuries ago.

7

Nazareth in England

Norfolk
11th to 15th century
2.3 kilometres (two miles)
Map: OS Explorer 251

Sometimes the only walk one wants is a very short walk. Sometimes it is good to have a walk, but one simply doesn't feel truly inclined to don the comfy but cumbersome boots and go for hours. Actually, I adore my walking boots. They are so very comfortable, and oddly comforting too. Heaven only knows why. Still, as I said – sometimes a short walk is just what one wants.

That is how I felt as I travelled from King's Lynn to Walsingham, one of the most visited and important pilgrimage sites in Europe – a hundred years or so before Canterbury, even. The Walsingham Shrine website says (in an of course biased and completely understandable way) that Walsingham was the more important of the two, since it is the Virgin Mary who was venerated there. Canterbury, on the other hand, had merely a saint. Be that as it may, both were destroyed in the 16th century during the Dissolution. Obviously, however, the power of prayer and pilgrimage is strong enough to cause a modern-day revival in the popularity of pilgrimages to this small village in a fairly empty part of a corner of the country. There are times when it is bursting at the seams.

Not today, though; I had it all to myself. Today, I decided on a circular walk. Setting off early, I drove down the narrow, winding roads of North Norfolk from my campsite near the Lynn. No one was about at this early hour except for the milk van hurtling towards me down the road as I frantically pulled out of its way, and I saw, too, a momentary flash of the postman's red van as it shot down a lane ahead. I parked up in the village of Little Walsingham itself, popping a few coins in the meter. It was still pretty early on an out-of-season weekday. Nice and quiet. I put on my boots, laced them nice and tight and pulled on my waterproof. The wind was wild, so I left off my hat; I could see myself chasing after it across the fields. The sky was marvellous: blue in patches with fluffy white clouds racing at breakneck speed overhead. No time for them to rest or cast a shadow, but here, down on the ground, it was pretty gusty. Anything not done up tight was flapping around, and I tripped over my stick more than once while walking along as a gust caught it and twisted it between my feet.

I strode off to the square named the Common Place in the centre of the village. Here was the bus stop, attached to the old Pump House right in the centre of a three-way split in the road. The Anglican Shrine, housing the replica of 'the holy house', was down to my left; the pub, hidden from my view by the Pump House, was in front of me; which in turn was in front of the site of the old abbey; and more or less to my right was the High Street. I wanted none of these options particularly; I was looking to get out of town on the Pilgrims' Way. That was slightly up the hill, sort of behind me as I stood there. I did walk down the High Street to begin with, gazing in the windows of the pilgrim shops. These, I presumed, had probably been pilgrims' hostels and inns rather than shops in medieval times, when things were really booming. They were full of statues of the Virgin Mary and Jesus, and rosaries, plus all other sorts of religious iconography. Some few metres down on my left I saw the monumental gate to the old grounds of the ruined Walsingham Abbey. To my right was the road into Friday Market Square with the Black Lion Hotel, the Catholic church and the Pilgrim Bureau. I walked in and through it, and went up Station Road.

This part of the village looked as though it could actually be in the 21st century, unlike the main part that appeared to be still stuck firmly in the Middle Ages. Station Road took me, obviously, to the station, but it is now disused, purged in the infamous Beeching cuts of the early 1960s. Here I was greeted with the sight of the delightful Russian Orthodox Chapel of St Seraphim at the top of the hill. A Russian Orthodox chapel had been built into the original Anglican Shrine when it was reconstructed in the 1930s, but subsequently, when the shrine's authorities asked the Orthodox Church to take responsibility for it, they decided to create their own space. So in 1966 they converted the old abandoned station building into a small chapel dedicated to Seraphim of Sarov, a great teacher of the Eastern Orthodox Church during the 18th century. Their other choice of building, apparently, had been an old prison. I think they made a good choice. The chapel is full of gorgeous traditional Russian icons. A railway station does still exist, by the way; it is a little way north of the old one and serves only the popular tourist steam train line from Wells-next-the-Sea.

To reach the path itself I crossed the large expanse of car park – where once the trains had stood is now painted with the outlines of where to park the huge coaches bringing in dozens of pilgrims. It is a beautifully easy path running parallel to the road below me. I had wondered if it would be muddy – it had rained quite hard the previous night – but no, the surface was stony and despite the odd puddle was pretty much dry. I could easily imagine a large crowd of pilgrims walking prayerfully down here, perhaps singing away joyfully. I imagine, too, that wheelchair users could manage this well enough; a rare thing for most pilgrim walks. Being alone allowed me to stop and gaze around for as long as I wanted. The wind was strong and refreshing, aka freezing, but I loved it. I felt cleansed by it – all cobwebs blown out and replaced by pleasing contentment. I stayed still to watch a couple of squabbling birds and a cock pheasant race from hedge to field and back to hedge. The sunshine appeared and disappeared at speed, racing across the newly ploughed fields. One minute it was bright and I had to squint, but then, moments later, it would be cloudy again. I walked on, thinking of old pilgrims and new.

It all began in 1061, five years before William the Conqueror beat Harold at the Battle of Hastings. The lady of the manor, Richeldis de Faverches, had a great devotion for the Virgin Mary and implored, in prayer, to be allowed a special task to deepen her worship. So in a dream she was taken to Nazareth by the Virgin and there shown Mary's home where she had been when the Archangel Gabriel had come to her. The Virgin Mary instructed Richeldis to build a replica of it as an everlasting memorial of the Annunciation.

Within fifty years the small (probably) wattle-and-daub building put up to represent the Nazarene house had become a major national shrine tended by a community of Augustinian canons. Every King of England from Henry III to Henry VIII, from 1226 to 1538, came to worship here, and not only the Kings of England but many others too. For hundreds of years pilgrims were drawn from all over England, Scotland and the Continent. They came into the ports such as King's Lynn, as I had, or perhaps the most famous route was the Palmer's Way, tracing the path from London. This was, more than likely, the one taken by two of the last royal pilgrims to visit. Two of Henry VIII's queens, Catherine of Aragon and Anne Boleyn, made the arduous journey. Erasmus, in 1513, made a pilgrimage from Cambridge and then wrote perhaps the best description of Walsingham from the time.

Then in 1538 it all came crashing down when King Henry VIII, in a political move, dissolved all religious houses and set himself up as the head of the Church of England. The priory was broken up; all the jewels and treasures gathered from centuries of pilgrims' offerings were either destroyed or taken off to London, including the statue of the Virgin Mary holding the Baby Jesus from the shrine itself. There it was reputedly burnt, along with other idolatrous images. The religious, the monks, nuns and priests were either pensioned off or, where they refused to accept the new truth, executed.

So as with all the rest of the religious houses throughout England, the priory was sold off and used as a manor house for anyone rich enough, or important enough, to own such a fine estate. Walsingham Priory was handed on until eventually it was sold to John Warner, the Bishop of Rochester. He then handed it over to his sister, who was called Lee. Her descendant's name became Lee Warner and the priory is still owned by the family, who are now called Gurney.

But perhaps the spirit of the Virgin Mary never really abandoned Walsingham, but simply became very quiet. Various publications that I read in preparation for this walk suggest that the Slipper Chapel, one mile from the shrine and the last chance to pray before reaching the final glory of the pilgrimage, continued to see people coming and praying.

I was on my way to the Slipper Chapel. The Pilgrim Path is the abandoned railway track, and hence is level and wide. It is surrounded on both sides by fields, and it is only at the end that there is a way off it. At that point, at the edge of the fields and at a track down to the road about fifty metres away, is the start of another path. This is the Rosary Way – a walk of peace, contemplation and prayer. It was unused just now but I could see a person coming up the hill to walk it, so I left them to their quiet space. After a gentle twenty-minute walk along the Pilgrim Path I came off it and walked down the track, and found myself right next to the Basilica of Our Lady of Walsingham, the Slipper Chapel, and the Chapel of Our Lady of Reconciliation.

This is a Catholic house of worship, the shrine with 'replica holy house' in the village is Anglican but both are places of deep devotion. The Slipper Chapel was built sometime in the 14th century. It was the final chapel where pilgrims could come and pray, say Mass and ask for forgiveness for their sins on their long journeys. This chapel, one mile short of their goal, would have held enormous significance. It was the place to pray for acceptance at the shrine, that Our Lady should hear their petition and grant them forgiveness through her intercession with Our Lord. Hence it may have been named the Slipper Chapel as it stood between normal, everyday life and the shrine where Our Lady was present: *Slype* is Old English for 'between'. Otherwise it is suggested that pilgrims would simply take off their slippers here and walk the rest of the way barefoot. The name has stuck, whatever its antecedents, and it is still the last house of prayer before the shrine of the Holy House. The chapel is dedicated to the patroness of all pilgrims, St Catherine, as she was the patron saint of the knights who protected pilgrims to the village of Nazareth in the Holy Land. The shrine at Walsingham is called England's Nazareth.

After the Dissolution, the chapel fell into semi-ruin and variously ended up as a cow barn and all sorts of other things, but according to stories told, at about the time of the rebuilding, people would still come to pray there. One man remembered some villagers talking of their great-grandfather being annoyed because these people would ask to pray in his cowshed. Its revival came in the 19th century when a woman called Charlotte Boyd managed to buy it. She had wanted to buy the shrine itself but was unsuccessful, so made do with purchasing the Slipper Chapel instead. She thought it would make a good convent. She was originally Anglican, but during a retreat in 1895 converted to Catholicism, becoming an oblate of Downside, the Benedictine monastery (promised to the monastery but not a professed member of the clergy who live in general society). She gave the chapel to Downside. It was a while before the first Mass since the Reformation was held there – that wasn't until 1934 and in that same year, Cardinal Francis Bourne led a ten-thousand-strong pilgrimage there and declared the chapel to be the Catholic national shrine of Our Lady.

Walking around the complex, I came first to the Chapel of Our Lady of Reconciliation. It is enormous and modern, all wood inside, and apparently built in the same architectural style as the Norfolk barns in the area. I was slightly taken aback by its size and uniformity of colour, as well as the power of the steel beams in the roof. But the focal point is the altar. All the pews bend towards it, and to the enormous glass window behind. This can be slid back, allowing the outside to come in, so to speak. There are times when the numbers of pilgrims are so great that the chapel is not big enough, and in these cases it can revert to being the open-air chapel it once was. The celebrant moves around the altar, then, and faces out. The window was closed for now. It has the most wonderful engravings swirling over it, emphasising the altar before it. The website for Walsingham (www.walsingham. org.uk) describes the altar as being made out of Aberdeen marble, and embedded within it are the relics of Saints Thomas of Canterbury, Laurence of Rome and the doctor of the Church in Henry VIII's time, Thomas More. There were a few people sitting or kneeling, praying before the altar, on which was a great monstrance with the body of Christ exposed, as it is before every noonday Mass. As I knelt to pray I couldn't help but be mesmerised by the simply huge TV screen above the altar. It depicts the Last Supper, Jesus and his disciples sitting at the last meal of his life, lit purely by candlelight. Personally, I found it rather overpowering.

Having stopped for a short while, I moved on and around the chapel into the Cloister Garden. Here were all the outdoor benches for the Masses said for big crowds of pilgrims, plus the Stations of the Cross. The oak crosses of the Stations were each carried from afar during the so-called Cross-Carrying Pilgrimage in 1948. There is a list of the places they came from and how far they were carried. Tucked away in the corner of the Cloister Garden I saw taps for holy water. Some people like to fill small bottles of blessed water to take home with them.

Down on the left at the end of the garden is the Slipper Chapel, now a minor basilica. There are two entrance doors, but a sign pointed me in the direction of the Door of Mercy. In December 2015 Pope Francis declared a jubilee year, the Holy Year of Mercy. The practice of jubilee years began in the 15th century and then meant a great journey to Rome, but this time Pope Francis wanted everyone to be able to experience the richness of the Holy Year. He declared that every diocesan cathedral could have a holy door, and that even local bishops could choose others too. The Slipper Chapel had, however, been awarded a great honour by Pope Francis just before the beginning of the Holy Year. He proclaimed the national shrine of Our Lady to be a minor basilica – one of only four in the country and 1,600 around the world. A minor basilica outranks all other churches except of course the major basilicas in Rome, and as such the shrine had its own holy door. The entrance was decorated very prettily with white and yellow roses, and as I pushed open the door I walked into the Chapel of the Holy Ghost and down a short corridor into the small space that is the chapel. It is all gold and blue, or at least that is what my initial impression was. It is very shiny. The statue of Our Lady holding the Baby Jesus sits on a throne with a white lily of peace. Jesus is cradling a book in his arms and they sit under a tall, ornate canopy. Behind the altar is a gold-and-blue reredos, and above it all is a vaulted ceiling with a central roundel depicting the Holy Spirit as the white dove of peace. The rest is also blue and gold. The small space is full of atmosphere and peace.

Passing out of the Chapel of the Holy Ghost, I passed by a statue of St Hugh of Lincoln. He is sometimes remembered as the bishop who bit off the finger of Mary Magdalene's relic at the abbey at Fécamp. He tried to break some off but it was too hard, so he used his teeth instead. Some strange deeds were done to get relics in the past. By the door is a list of the relics contained within this shrine. It includes the bones of eighteen saints, beginning with St Catherine of Siena and ending with Pope John Paul II, who died in 2005. Just next to the chapel are the shop and the administrative offices, plus the café of course. There were masses of things on display in the shop: shelves with lots of books from the lives of the saints to Bibles; rosaries of every shape, colour and size; medals and medallions; lapel pins; and fridge magnets too, of a small Virgin Mary with Jesus, seated on her throne.

However, the walk was only half done, so time to carry on. This time I was returning on the road itself. This is not the safest route, of course, but is not very busy so with care, and as long as you keep listening for the hum of a motor and the rush of car tyres, it is safe enough. This is the Holy Mile, the route that the original pre-car pilgrims would always have used. The Pilgrim Path above is just to keep us safe, but this is the more 'authentic' path. The hedge is pretty high on both sides and the path a bit narrow for cars and walkers, but soon the small lane to the Catholic shrine joins the main road, Fakenham Road, which is slightly wider and busier. I walked on and I think I encountered only three cars. Of course the road is closed for the main pilgrimage processions. Here I was walking below my previous route, which I could see as a treeline on the hill to my left, and on my right (but mostly not visible) was the River Stiffkey. Walking on, I could imagine medieval pilgrims spotting the village for the first time and realising how close it was. Soon they would be finishing what may have been a long and difficult journey.

As you come into the bottom of the village, it is a gentle slope uphill, up the High Street. As the road forked I walked past the red-brick perimeter wall of the Coachman's House which I couldn't see as the wall was too high, but on my left I stopped at a gate. A sign told me I was at the entrance of what was once a Franciscan priory, and is now simply a pile of ruins. A Methodist chapel stands in its stead, and both are on private land. The further up the High Street one goes the more shops there are, including the Pilgrim Gift Shop with everything on display. As I walked up to Common Place I knew the grounds of

Walsingham Abbey were just to my right, behind the row of houses. The entrance to the grounds is through the museum next to the Bull Inn in the Common Place, but I was on my way to the Anglican Shrine so I walked past the museum and the pub and into the modern-looking building – all pale pine and clean. The complex is large. There are many different facets to it and I wasn't sure what to see first, but of course I was drawn to the Nazarene house, or at least its modern-day replica.

Father Patten rebuilt the shrine in the 1930s, after the Bishop of Norfolk ordered him to take down an image of the Virgin Mary from his parish church in Walsingham. In response, Father Patten looked for the money to buy a plot of land in Walsingham and build a small church to recreate the replica Nazarene house. He was successful, and his little church has had to be enlarged many times to accommodate all the people visiting since then. Within the shrine church stands not only the Holy House, but also a well that was found during the original construction. Father Patten was delighted and believed the waters had healing powers. As I entered the church I saw the steps down to the well in front of the tomb of Father Patten himself. Pilgrims can step down one side of the well, be sprinkled with holy water by a priest and then ascend the other side – this leads to a non-stop queue of pilgrims. Also within the enlarged building (in other words not part of the original) are fifteen chapels, all dedicated to a particular saint and named after the Mysteries of the Rosary.

As I wandered about I did feel a bit confused by it all, but then I turned into the Holy House itself. It is lit only by the light of dozens of candles, except for the altar. This blazes with light and colour. In front is a low dais on which is a fine Persian rug. The base of the altar is gold with two angels holding a medallion of the Christogram IHS, and above on the altar itself stand four tall candles in superb silver candelabrum Behind them is a frieze with three scenes from the life of the Virgin Mary, but it is above this that one's eye is taken. Here is a statue of the Virgin holding the Baby Jesus, and again the lily of peace.

She is crowned with a splendid gold circlet, but about her shoulders is a truly magnificent cape. Fully and beautifully embroidered, it is spread out in its glory to form a sort of triangle, and a gold canopy surmounts all of this. To add to the magnificence of the statue, a golden frame with radiating beams surrounds it, as if light is flowing out of the statue. With the rest of the interior in semi-darkness, it stands out quite powerfully.

Coming out of the Holy House I found my bearings and walked around the chapels. I found the beautiful ceramic of the Annunciation. I love its serenity and the simplicity of it, but then I came across the Chapel of the Ascension. I have to admit that I was amazed. In the ceiling was a sort of ceiling rose, and ascending into Heaven through it were the ceramic soles of the feet of Jesus. This was art from another age and I tried to take it seriously, but it is just not my style. I wasn't keen on a statue of the Blessed Virgin Mary with a dagger through her heart either. Others love these sorts of slightly maudlin statues, but I find them mildly depressing, though it is just a matter of preference.

I wandered out soon after and restored my feeling of calm with a visit to the Sepulchre. This is a replica of the tomb where Jesus was laid and from which he rose from the dead. This was again very lovely and simple. All tastes are different. The gardens, however, are serene beauty itself. They are landscaped to provide different areas of quiet serenity and mediation. The central one is dominated by the three crosses of Calvary, built on a mound to represent that the area of Calvary was raised. It is an interesting visual gesture that makes one looks up at the three crosses of the Crucifixion. On a mound next to the Calvary crosses, on the upper lawn, is the open-air altar named the Altar of the Mysteries of Light, which was built in 2005. Again, as with the Chapel of Reconciliation at the Catholic shrine, large pilgrimages would hear Mass surrounding the altar outside rather than crowding into the space of the shrine church. The Serpentine Path leads one around the different areas of the garden – to areas of prayer and peace, but principally from the shrine church to the upper lawn and Calvary.

Spending hours wandering about was quite timeless, and then having a look at the exhibitions in the visitor centre, it was very easy to lose oneself for ages. Eventually though I knew the money would be running out in my parking meter and hence it was time to be on my way. A fascinating day with a nice walk included.

8

Chaucer's Canterbury Trail

(After a fashion, and not in their footsteps at all)

Kent

Medieval

Ninety-five kilometres

Maps: OS Explorer 148, 149, 150, 162, 163, 173

Geoffrey Chaucer's *Canterbury Tales* was written in the middle of 14th century. I read it while at school, but I admit the Old English language defeated me. It was years later that I had another go and read a modern English version and realised it was extraordinary. Chaucer still has ardent fans and I think he was a bestseller then too, and I have no doubt whatsoever that his *Tales* did inspire people to take that path of pilgrimage to Canterbury. Maybe they went for the fun of it – a bit of a holiday – or maybe they went as true penitential pilgrims. What people hold in their thoughts, in their heads, is their business, but whatever their reasons, it was indeed a veritable highway down to the Augustine city of Canterbury.

As with very many pilgrim routes, there appear to be several different ways to reach the 'destination'. Most pilgrims were believed to gather at the Tabard Inn on Borough High Street, nearby to the still-standing, almost original George Inn. The George still has its medieval courtyard where coaches would have left for all parts of England or the coast, and those arriving that would have disgorged their passengers before they could cross Southwark Bridge and on into London. People now gather there – sometimes with a pint or a coffee – before marching out, staff in hand, to forge down the streets to the Old Kent Road and out to the Kent countryside. But it was not to seek out the relics of St Augustine that pilgrims in Chaucer's time travelled from far and wide. It was to the shrine of St Thomas Becket, and they came in their droves.

I started walking in the town of Dartford, not from the George; Borough High Street is very busy. Dartford is about twenty-five kilometres away from Borough High Street. Historically it is regarded as the first night's stopping place, a good day's walk from Southwark. I arrived in the early-morning sunshine and hoped to go into the church for a prayer to start my day, but it was far too early and it was still locked up. The cleaner came out while I was standing by the door, but she was rushing for her breakfast, so I couldn't ask her to wait for me. Instead, I set off immediately, heading away southward. Unlike Chaucer's pilgrims I didn't have to think up a story to tell and be judged on, thankfully. I had the solitude to think my own thoughts, savour the fresh morning air and relish the quiet. There were, unlike on most of my walks, more people hereabouts. I walked through the town's park and found the gardeners quietly digging and weeding. Runners were doing their thing and a few dog owners were silently walking in the dewy grass. The path is very easy here, through and out of Dartford – through the park, past the council chambers, following the River Darent, and that then joins the path of the Darent Valley Way. The path is well signposted and I did follow it most of the day.

It is almost impossible to follow the route that Chaucer's people would have walked. Today roads, railway tracks, houses, offices and industrial estates unfortunately swallow it up. Hedges, fences, gardens and barriers of all descriptions force one onto the major roads. Why do that? I was in St Augustine's Church in Ramsgate, Augustus Pugin's family church. As I wandered about looking at the stained-glass windows and reliquaries (including one of St Augustine himself), I found in the church porch several interesting books and DVDs, including one of a pilgrimage that the parish priest, Father Holden, had walked of a route from London to Canterbury, on a quite different road to the usual. This one took him and his companion away from busy places and into the countryside; a much closer experience to the original, and one I much preferred.

The River Darent would have been quite a problem for pilgrims of bygone ages, but a nearby helpful hermit used to ferry them across apparently. Now, sadly, I didn't have any hermits to hand, but the river is tamed – there are bridges. I walked along a well-made footpath that also doubles as a convenient flood control, and through a low tunnel that had pretty twinkly lights, as well as rather nice classical music playing gently. The music is apparently to stop young people from hanging about, as it seems they hate classical music. Ah, I must be old now as I rather enjoyed it.

Along the Darent, just past the tunnel, are a couple of largish patches of water called the Brookland Lakes that have been formed out of gravel pits. During the Second World War they were covered with nets to camouflage them as the Vickers munitions factory was pretty close and the lakes could have been used as a location beacon when bombing the factory. Now they're a haven for wildlife and a paradise for anglers. It was still deserted as I walked past except for the birds dipping and diving in the early morning.

The further I got from Dartford town, the rougher the path became until the concrete stopped and I was back on bare earth, following the undulating bends of the river. I was still passing some industrial areas, but at least not actually walking through them. A nice alternative. I made a detour a couple of kilometres down the track to stop in the village of Sutton-at-Hone. Here, a commandry of the Knights Hospitallers of the Order of St John of Jerusalem was set up in 1199. The chapel of the commandry still exists and is open to the public once a week in the summer. It's a wonderful place; just a small room up a few steps, with wooden floors, whitewashed walls, tall lancet windows, and a few sparse pieces of dark oak furniture. Of course, the altar is dominant in the room, and even though it's not actually a chapel any more, it could easily be again. The red altar cloth draped over the altar is emblazoned with the eight-pointed cross of St John of Jerusalem (which is also the cross of the Knights of Malta). The chapel is on the side of a beautiful house – not open to the public, but the gardens are, and when I was there in high summer, the flowers were quite marvellous. The Darent River runs almost all the way around the house and creates a sort of mini-moat, giving it a very Crusader-ish atmosphere.

Back on the track and back to earth, I walked through the village of South Darenth and passed through Horton Kirby, constantly following the river, walking towards the noise of the M20 motorway, which I ducked under to find myself in Farningham, near to the charming red-brick Lion Hotel. But not much was going on here (mid morning and no one to be seen), so I walked on through the village and turned left to walk down Sparepenny Lane, hoping to see something of Eynsford Castle.

I almost missed it entirely. I simply forgot all about it, in the pleasure of walking! There I was, loving putting one foot in front of the other, musing about life, the sky and the calling birds, and how beautiful the countryside was. I thought of Chaucer's pilgrims and tried to recall some of their stories. All I could remember, though, were the overly pious knights who spent their time questing for love. There are worse quests to pursue, to be sure. I thought too of how Protestantism put an end, more or less, to pilgrimage. The Protestants saw the displaying of relics and the kissing of bones as idolatrous and just a way to bring in money. Only two places continued to attract pilgrims. One was Our Lady's shrine at Walsingham and the other the shrine of St Winefride at Holywell in Wales. However, they never again received as many as in previous times and pilgrimage became more or less a secretive thing to do. So I only glanced at the castle, and thought, *Oh well, I'll stop off and see Lullingstone Castle instead, just up the road.*

But just up the road, I found the Lullingstone Roman villa rather than the castle. A brilliant place to stop for a while, and I couldn't resist going in. The displays are wonderfully done and it was fascinating. I walked around the ruins on a raised walkway, so I could see the layout of the villa. The Romans did well for themselves, judging by the luxury of this home. Of course this would have been a notably rich area; not only because of the rich soil for growing crops, but also being so near the coast and France for trading. The information displayed described such detail of the place, and archaeologists have found such treasures there too. I spent far too long staring through the glass panels at broken pots and homely tools. Thankfully, I was chased out by the arrival of two coachloads of schoolchildren. Not only were there hordes of them but the noise was ear-shattering too, and I really did need to move on anyway.

So now I expected Lullingstone Castle to be almost next door, but it's not. I had to walk about a kilometre or so down the road before I came to it, and sadly it was closed; quite shut up. So that was it for castles! The river made up for my disappointment as it was a particularly pretty walk down on the banks. I did have to shimmy my way by another class of schoolkids who were out for a nature lesson; lots of kids and a narrow path. It amused me that the poor teacher was trying so hard to control the lads: "Do put on your wellies before you get in the river, Peter" and "No, don't splash the girls, Michael!" I smiled a sympathetic smile when I reached her in a sort of grown-up kinship. She raised her eyes to Heaven and sighed. I laughed and moved on.

By the time I made it to Shoreham, it was definitely worth a sit-down as the next town was Otford, and from there a whole new chapter of the walk would begin. At Otford the track turns left and joins up with the North Downs Way, aka the Pilgrims' Way, all the way from Winchester to Canterbury. It felt like an old friend! I had walked many miles since I had followed this almost venerable path before. I remembered a fine tea room on this street from the last time I was here, but was so disappointed to see the place closed and the windows dirty. Further up around the village pond the cafés were thriving still, thank goodness. I ended my first day here and was happy to sit down and reflect on a cheery day.

My next stretch took me from Otford over to nearby Kemsing. I decided to make this a little side-walk – it's only about a kilometre away from Otford. For pilgrims it was a pretty important place. Here is the Church of St Mary the Virgin, and also the site of a monastery founded by St Edith of Wilton.

Edith was the illegitimate daughter of King Edgar I, the Peaceful, and was born in 961. Histories of Edgar tell the story of him abducting Edith's mother Wilfrida from her convent in Wilton, and taking her to Kemsing where she gave birth. They called their daughter Edith, or Eadgyth in Anglo-Saxon. Wilfrida returned to the convent with her baby, but she and Edgar remained on good terms, it seems. He supported her convent until his death when Edith was fourteen years old. St Dunstan, who was the Archbishop of Canterbury at the time, meted out a penance of sorts to Edgar for his sacrilege of abducting a woman from a place of sanctuary, and instructed him not to wear his crown for seven years. Edith's half-brother, Edward the Martyr, became king on Edgar's death, but was murdered soon after by his stepmother. Edith is said to have had a dream before the murder in which she had lost her right eye, and this, she believed, foretold Edward's death. It is rumoured that the crown was offered to her following his death, but as a novice nun she (very sensibly, considering her brother's end) refused.

Edith died in 984 at the age of twenty-three and several miracles were reported very soon after. The medieval writer Goscelin, who wrote her hagiography, wrote that St Dunstan himself opened Edith's tomb some thirteen years after her death. Her body was found to be uncorrupted and a *perfume of paradise* emanated from the tomb. Unfortunately for this story we know that Dunstan died four years after her, so the dates don't quite match up. Edith became famous in medieval times as the patron saint of eyes, and her well in the centre of the village of Kemsing became a great focus for pilgrims with any sort of eye complaint. Chaucer's pilgrims might have taken a detour for this holy well.

Father Holden's DVD mentions another story of Kemsing, but this time connected to the Church of St Mary the Virgin. It concerns the four knights who murdered St Thomas Becket. A legend (of which there are very many) says that they passed through here on their way to the cathedral at Canterbury that dark, cold night and, on the anniversary of the murder (29th December), a single knight wearing his armour and riding his horse is seen entering the church. He dismounts and kneels before the altar as though asking for forgiveness for his terrible crime before gradually fading away for another year.

My detour to St Edith's Well was still very close to the waymarked pilgrim route, which then took me high onto the edge of the scarp by Otford Manor again, and along the fields and lanes to Wrotham. Here the signs pointing the direction for the Pilgrims' Way appear more often than those for the North Downs Way. Again, I felt a deep kinship walking in the footsteps of those I believe had walked here for so many centuries until Henry's Dissolution outlawed it. Not far past Trottiscliffe, just north of Birling, I left the marked Pilgrims' Way and walked east. Normally the route goes northwards from here and on into the city of Rochester on the River Medway. This I'd done on my previous walk; this time, however, I wanted to go on to Aylesford Priory instead. It wasn't that easy to find a good route, as the public footpath signs were sparse. But if you head directly east from Birling to Horn Street and Ham Hill, cross over the Leybourne Lakes Country Park into Larkfield Trading Estate, and get over to the east bank of the Medway before joining up with the Medway Valley Walk, you can find lots of signs indicating the entrance to the priory.

This Aylesford Priory, as it is now, is fairly new, less than a century old, but it has history. Called The Friars and located in the heart of Kent, the monks first founded a monastery here in the 13th century but had to abandon it, or rather the Dissolution forced them into exile. In 1949 the house came up for sale and fortunately the order was able to buy it back, and so the Carmelite mother house was restored. The Carmelite order is unlike most other religious orders in that it has no founder. It is believed it grew out of the community of hermit monks who lived and prayed on the slopes of Mount Carmel in the Holy Land near the Well of Elijah. They were given land at Aylesford by the Crusader knight Richard de Grey in his manor at Aylesford, and from there they spread throughout England and the Continent, changing from hermit monks to mendicant friars (begging brothers).

Since 1949 the priory has been a major centre of pilgrimage. It is in a truly beautifully place in an outstanding setting. The old buildings provide accommodation for those on retreat, as well as a fine 12th-century hall that is now the Pilgrims Hall Restaurant. The open arena, created in 1949, is an open-air church with four chapels in a semicircle around the seating area. Huge groups come in for retreat days and Mass can be said outside with all the doors open, or more intimately in one of the chapels. In one is a reliquary with part of the skull of St Simon Stock, one of their prior generals who was canonised. According to the stories, the Virgin Mary appeared to him and gave him a brown scapular, a sort of apron. It's now part of the habit of the order, usually a small piece of cloth worn hidden beneath the outer clothes.

The avenue into the priory led between lovely large oaks, silhouetted with the sunlight shining through, low as it was late afternoon when I arrived. It was very inviting; I really did feel it was asking me in. It wasn't busy, but a few people were wandering about. Some were families walking through the grounds. Some were in the adjacent café drinking cups of tea, and some were praying in the chapels. I went to the reception and had a lovely chat with one of the brothers, who had had a late vocation and converted to become a friar. He spoke with great joy of his life and optimistic hope for the future. I came out with a cheerful smile and renewed energy.

Away from Aylesford it's a bit of cross-country to reach the Way again, so I took a bus to Detling to meet up with the route from there. I'd walked this way before so it was a familiar path, but interesting to see it changed on a sunny and dry day – for the most part. From Detling the track reaches back up to the scarp and follows the edge all the way until it drops down to Hollingbourne, where I walked past The Dirty Habit pub again and carried on along the Pilgrims' Way. It was a dry day – the sun was warm on my face, the wheat was ripe for harvesting in the fields, and the hedges were brimming with nettles and brambles. I found a small handwritten sign pinned to a tree that warned passers-by of an outbreak of hairy caterpillars, which could give one a rash. I pulled in my elbows and swung my stick a little less vigorously.

Several of the tracks had a good amount of standing water on them, usually not too deep thankfully, but I was wearing wellies because of the recent rain. The gravel surface soon ran out, but the path continued as a good wide track. Unfortunately, in some places vehicles (tractors or quad bikes) had gouged quite deep ruts. On the way between Hollingbourne and Harrietsham I found myself facing a huge puddle that I couldn't see the bottom of. There was nowhere to walk alongside it and no way of walking around in the field, so I probed the depth with my walking stick and felt only slippery mud. It was too deep to walk through – I reckoned it was way over the tops of my boots. I could just about see a rise in the level of the mud, and I tried to reach it. I failed and ended up sliding into the puddle up to my waist! I was actually lying in the water, on my side, trying to keep my phone in my pocket dry. I didn't mind being wet but the problem was that if I moved I would slip in more deeply, as I had no foothold at all in the mud. So I dug my stick in (losing the rubber end in the process) and levered myself out gingerly. My only emotion was regret that I didn't have anyone to have a really good laugh with! So I sat down on a convenient fallen tree and, having strained and struggled to pull my wellies off (suction), I phoned a friend and laughed.

And what I real mess I was then. Covered in drying mud, mud streaked on my face too, and a horrible squelching noise from my boots as I walked. I had to smile. I met a few ladies out walking with their dogs a kilometre or so further on and they asked me what happened – they were most sympathetic and laughed loudly too. Not much later I came across an immaculately dressed walker; straight out of a catalogue. Firstly, it is so rare to come across another real walker with backpack and sticks, so that was different. Secondly, she was just so scrupulously clean. Even without the mud-sucking puddles of my recent walk I would never have been able to stay that clean. She was wearing a pale green T-shirt, a short beige skirt, white ankle socks and her boots were clean too. Did she float? She wasn't very chatty and when we talked I realised that a) she wasn't English (I thought Dutch or Scandinavian; she didn't say much), and b) the look on her face as she beheld me was pretty condescending – she was obviously thinking that anyone walking in wellies couldn't be taken seriously, and when I warned her of the danger ahead she was very dismissive. I was quite tempted to follow her and see what she did with the puddle. I didn't, though, and watched her stride off with a chuckle.

Such adventures raised my spirits even higher and I walked into Charing with pleasure and had a quick look in the church again. I thought I'd try and see the stone on which John the Baptist was beheaded. It was apparently brought back from the Crusades, and the last time I was here I had completely forgotten about it. I searched the church and even asked a couple of other people if they had seen it, but nothing. They did look at my filthy clothes with puzzled faces until I explained my mishap whereupon we had a laugh together. But back to the stone I thought perhaps the church authorities had hidden out of sight – it was a gruesome memento of the Holy Land anyway, and relics are not really acceptable any longer.

So, the delightful village of Charing again – this is where the pilgrims would gather so as not to walk through the King's Wood alone, and be safe in numbers, but no one else turned up so I simply walked on through the wood. I have to admit that it would have been nice to walk with another person here as the wood goes on and on for miles with nothing to look at but trees. I still failed to spot a wild boar – I think they are just a story after all. Eventually I walked into Chilham and on into the apple orchards on the other side of the village. It was all very much as I remembered, although now it wasn't raining, which was nice. Such a comfortable path. I even remembered what I was thinking about as I came this way before! I seem to remember I thought about stealing apples.

Coming into Canterbury this time was quite a different experience. It wasn't the route, but how I felt. I did take the time, this time, to duck down again into the Pilgrims' Hospital and stand still for a short while, to centre myself and enjoy the experience, before coming out and turning right down the High Street and left into Mercery Lane. Then slowly I made my way through the marvellous and enormous Christ Church Gate. This time I didn't announce myself as a pilgrim but said that I had come simply to pray. The man at the ticket kiosk waved me through and I slipped in past all the sightseers. I didn't go to the front entrance, but walked around to the back of the cathedral. Here, I knew, was the doorway into the cloister that the four murdering knights had flung open, before running down and then bursting through into the side chapel, straight to where Archbishop Thomas was saying Mass in the cathedral. Surrounded by his brother monks, they struck him down and he died where he fell on that cold, wintry night of 29th December 1170.

I made my way down to the undercroft and found the sculpture by Antony Gormley that hangs over the spot where the original shrine stood – where Thomas' shocked and horrified brother monks laid his dead body – until the splendid and magnificent shrine was built in the main body of the cathedral, exactly above here, only for that to be destroyed, much like St Thomas himself.

So, here I was for the second time, the second in the cathedral and the third in Canterbury, at the end of a pilgrim walk. I found an 'authentic' pilgrim's badge for sale in the cathedral shop. It is an exact replica of one of the original badges created during the Middle Ages for pilgrims to carry home as a souvenir. It depicts the magnificent shrine of St Thomas and shows his body lying at its centre, surrounded by canopies and offerings. The shrine was covered in priceless jewels. They were all over the reliquary, and on the replica badge, above the prone figure of St Thomas, is a small monk's figure. It points to the gigantic ruby that was given by the French King Louis VII as a gift – no doubt so his soul would be cleansed by his benefaction. The ruby was reputed to be the largest precious stone in the world, and its worth was said to be beyond measure. It ended up, of course, in a splendid ring made for King Henry VIII. I have it now – the replica badge, sadly not the jewel – as my souvenir of a lovely walk.

The circle is rounded – I started in Canterbury and finished in Canterbury, but there are so many more miles to be walked here on this fair island – in Scotland, Wales and England and then even more on the island of Ireland both North and South. These are just a few of the wonderful ancient routes we have to explore. To walk over the landscape and to know something of what went on before – to add people to the place.

Bibliography

Balding, Clare: *Walking Home: My Family and Other Rambles*. Penguin, 11th September 2014. Kindle edition.

The Benedictine nuns: *Minster Abbey: A Short Historical and Architectural Guide*. St Mildred's Abbey, Minster, Kent.

Cousineau, Phil: *The Art of Pilgrimage: The Seeker's Guide to Making Travel Sacred*. Conari Press, 1st August 2012. Kindle anniversary edition.

Cracknell, Linda: *Doubling Back: Ten Paths Trodden in Memory*. Freight Books, 26th May 2014. Kindle edition.

Dalladay, J.: *Hild of the Headlands: The Story of Hilda of Whitby*. 2016.

Eckersley, Nancy and John, with Comer, Mark: *Walking St Hilda's Way*. Mulgrave Community Research Project, 2014.

Farmer, David: *The Oxford Dictionary of Saints*. OUP, 1st January 2011. Fifth Kindle edition, revised (Oxford Quick Reference).

Foothpath Series: *The Saints' Way*. Yellow Publications, 2016

Gooley, Tristan: *The Natural Explorer: Understanding Your Landscape*.

Sceptre, 15th March 2012. Kindle edition.

Gooley, Tristan: *The Natural Navigator*. Virgin Digital, 30th March 2010. Kindle edition.

Hampshire County Council: *Saint Swithun's Way*.

Harrison, Melissa: *Rain: Four Walks in English Weather*. Faber & Faber, 1st March 2016. Kindle edition.

Hegge, Robert, and Webb, Simon: *The Legend of St Cuthbert: In A Modern English Version*. The Langley Press, 6th June 2013. Kindle edition.

Lewis, Heulyn L. and Ginny: *The Saints' Way: Walk Across Cornwall, Coast to Coast in the Footsteps of the Celtic Saints Forth an Syns*. Pelican Studio, Looe, Cornwall, 2012.

Macfarlane, Robert: *Landmarks*. Penguin, 5th March 2015. Kindle edition.

Merrill, the Revd. John N.: *Bury St. Edmunds to Walsingham: 77 Mile Pilgrimage Walk to Little Walsingham* (Pilgrim Walks Series no. 24). The John Merrill Ministry.

Phillips, Father Andrew: *The Hallowing of England: A Guide to the Saints of Old England and their Places of Pilgrimage*. Anglo-Saxon Books, Hockwold cum Wilton, Norfolk, 1994.

Ramirez, Janina: *The Private Lives of the Saints: Power, Passion and Politics in Anglo-Saxon England*. Virgin Digital, 27th August 2015. Kindle edition.

Rollings, Peter: *Walsingham: England's Nazareth*. R.C. National Shrine, Walsingham.

Rudd-Jones, Nicholas, and Stewart, David: *Pathways: Journeys Along Britain's Historic Byways*. Walkingworld Ltd, 29th September 2015. Kindle edition.

Saunders, Colin: *North Downs Way* (Official National Trail Guide). Aurum Press, in association with Walk Unlimited, 2013.

Sumption, Jonathan: *Pilgrimage*. Faber & Faber, 7th July 2011. Kindle edition.

Tavinor, David: *Shrines of the Saints: in England and Wales*. Canterbury Press, 28th February 2016. Kindle edition.

Turnbull, Ronald: *St Cuthbert's Way: From Melrose to Lindisfarne.* Rucksack Readers, Dunblane, 2010.

Ure, Sir John: *Pilgrimages: The Great Adventure of the Middle Ages.* Constable, February 2003. Hardback edition.

Wells, Emma J.: *Pilgrim Routes of the British Isles.* The Crowood Press, 31st August 2016. Kindle edition.

DVD: *To be a Pilgrim* with Father Marcus Holden and Father Nicholas Schofield. Produced and directed by Christian Holden, St Anthony Communications (www.saintant.com), 2015.